Praise for
The Inclusive Classroom

'Practical, concrete advice peppered with brilliant anecdotes. This utterly readable book is not just for teachers of children with SEND; it has the power to absolutely change the way every teacher approaches every child.'

Charlie Allison, SEND Lead at the Xavier Catholic Education Trust, consultant and lecturer

'It's rare to come across an educational book that I both wish I'd written and wish I'd read at the beginning of my career. *The Inclusive Classroom* is exactly such a book. It is packed with practical, relevant and insightful advice that will enable any classroom practitioner to really meet the needs of all their children. What I love most is its simplicity. Complex theory and years of knowledge are distilled into bite-sized tips that everyone, from new teachers to experienced leaders, can apply immediately to support the creation of a calm, secure learning environment for all. This should be essential reading on initial teacher training if we're serious as a nation about ensuring every child gets the education they deserve whilst giving teachers more precious time.'

Sarah Bailey, Headteacher of Croydon Virtual School and former primary school headteacher, @SarahBa19844848

'*The Inclusive Classroom* is essential reading for new and experienced teachers. It is insightful, accessible and packed with practical ideas.'

Dr Helen Curran, Senior Lecturer in SEN at Bath Spa University, @drhelcurran

'An honest, genuine and authentic read by two authors with personal, first-hand experience of SEN. The book is peppered with tangible ways to look to the needs of all children as individuals. The "Try this… Instead of this" sections are particularly useful for practitioners. I highly recommend it.'

Helen Frostick, former headteacher and educational consultant

'This book is a comprehensive, step-by-step guide for professionals on how to best create a well-balanced and supportive classroom. It's a must-read to improve your planning and delivery of lessons and take a holistic approach to SEN.'

Alice Green, primary school teacher, @mrsalicegreen

'This is a practical, honest and supportive guide to illuminate the importance of establishing an inclusive environment where all children can shine, be engaged and love their learning journey. It supports teachers to take structured steps to improve inclusivity for all children in their care. This is a must-read for every teacher and school leader!'

Stephen Lawler-Smith, National Leader of Education and Headteacher of Moorside Community Primary School, Salford

'*The Inclusive Classroom* urges us to really know what makes each young person in our care tick in order to support their learning. This is a must-have for everyone who works in schools.'

Jez Piper, CEO of Diocese of Bristol
Academies Trust, @DBAT_UK

'*The Inclusive Classroom* provides the perfect blend of tried and tested pedagogy with a fantastic and easily accessible way to advise all educators on how to be more inclusive. I thoroughly enjoyed the pearls of wisdom shared by two passionate educators who are refreshingly open and honest about the challenges they face with their own learning difficulties.'

Baasit Siddiqui, Director of Siddiqui Education, @SiddiquiEdu

'Dispelling myths, generously sharing their own personal experiences of the education system and breaking their helpful advice into easily applicable chunks, Daniel and Sara empower and enable teachers to make a difference to children's outcomes and life chances.'

Leanne Symonds, Headteacher and National Leader for Education,
Ringwood School and the SPELL Alliance

'Each and every pupil is both unique and special. An additional learning need is not necessarily a difficulty. This book provides a timely, personal and welcome reminder of the importance of individual pupils' needs, instead of an obsession with a diagnosis.'

Allison Yarrow, Deputy Headteacher and Wellbeing and
Achievement Lead, Cardiff High School, @AllisonYarrow

The Inclusive Classroom

A new approach to differentiation

Daniel Sobel and Sara Alston

BLOOMSBURY EDUCATION

LONDON OXFORD NEW YORK NEW DELHI SYDNEY

BLOOMSBURY EDUCATION
Bloomsbury Publishing Plc
50 Bedford Square, London, WC1B 3DP, UK
29 Earlsfort Terrace, Dublin 2, Ireland

BLOOMSBURY, BLOOMSBURY EDUCATION and the Diana logo are trademarks of
Bloomsbury Publishing Plc

First published in Great Britain, 2021 by Bloomsbury Publishing Plc

A catalogue record for this book is available from the British Library

ISBN: PB: 978-1-4729-7792-2; ePDF: 978-1-4729-7789-2; ePub: 978-1-4729-7790-8

8 10 9 7 (paperback)

Typeset by Newgen KnowledgeWorks Pvt. Ltd., Chennai, India
Printed and bound in the UK by CPI Group Ltd, Croydon CR0 4YY

To find out more about our authors and books visit www.bloomsbury.com
and sign up for our newsletters

Contents

Acknowledgements

I wrote this book to help better our world for the next generation and I dedicate it to my personal next generation: my children, Boaz, Toby and Abi, and my nieces and nephew, Leora, Gavriel, Zahava and Adina. I have genuinely tried my best to contribute something valuable and helpful to better our world somehow. I did it for all of us, but I did it with you in my heart.

I should say one of the most important thank yous and 'without you this would never have happeneds' to the ever so patient, deeply inspiring and utterly brilliant Sara Alston. Of course, it takes two to tango, but it's like you arranged the music, got the hall, designed the choreography and did everything else in between. Despite my frustrating you with missed deadlines and cancelled Zoom calls, I have learned a lot, a heck of a lot, from you, and I enjoyed slogging up this killer mountain together!

I always mention my core team, wherever I am and to whomever will listen. I do this because they are my bedrock and without them I would be nowhere. I absolutely love working with you guys. Thank you, my colleagues-friends-family, Sharon, Ren and Gosha.

A very special thanks to my sister Kate Gerstler for some very patient and clever editing of this book: and boy, did my contributions in particular need her wisdom, experience and frankly, intuition!

I'm not sure I would have done this all without the help of Hannah Marston at Bloomsbury, who is super-smashing-great-fun and warm, encouraging, clear and guiding. She is the perfect nudger that an author needs; three cheers for Hannah the Great.

My efforts are only a small element of my productivity. I'm supported, far more than anyone would ever expect, by my wonderful wife. I owe her everything. Unless one day we get divorced, in which case I owe her half. But I love her endlessly and she is my rock, not just to bash with me, but to uphold me every day, in facing any and every storm, in being the stable platform for my life. I owe her everything (or half if necessary).

Daniel Sobel

No book is the work of just one or, in this case, two people. It is a team effort involving many people, some of whom are conscious of their role and some of whom are unconscious of it. I want to start by thanking my co-author Daniel for his inspiration and big-picture vision. We are an odd partnership incorporating two very different work styles – lastminute.com compared with 'get everything in a week ahead of time'. But we managed to work together in reasonably good humour and without killing each other, possibly thanks to the COVID-19 lockdown, which meant much of our writing was done online. Thank you, Daniel, I couldn't have done it without you.

We have been ably supported by Hannah Marston at Bloomsbury. Also, by the amazing Inclusion Expert back office team. Special mentions should go to Sharon Finn, who coordinated diaries and ensured Daniel made most of our meetings, and Jude Farshi, who worked with me on the online courses I wrote for Inclusion Expert, which laid the foundation of the approach Daniel and I developed in this book. Thanks to Deborah Lewis, Kate Gerstler, Joshua Alston and others who have read different versions of the book, commented and helped with the editing. The mistakes remain mine and Daniel's.

Behind this are the many teams I have been part of over the years, all of whom have fed into this book in different ways. The Inclusion Expert consultants team are a wonderful group of educational experts who are a constant source of support, inspiration and challenge. Over the last 30-plus years, I have worked in a range of schools that have enabled me to form, develop, practise and refine my ideas about learning and teaching. All the staff, parents and children have contributed to this book in some way. I would like to thank particularly my colleagues and the families at Pyrcroft, Leatherhead Trinity and Pirbright Village Primary Schools and the multi-agency teams in Surrey, particularly the EPs, Specialist Teacher Team, SALTs, social workers and safeguarding trainers I have worked with.

In this book, we have included the stories of many children. All of these are fictional, though the inspiration comes from the children I have had the privilege to teach, who have probably taught me more than I have taught them.

I would like to thank particularly and dedicate this book to the female educators who believed in me when I didn't believe in myself: my mother Janice Rich, my great aunt Sarita Ricardo, Margaret Riddell, Jennifer Pullig, Rabbi Julia Neuberger, Meg Gibbons and Brenda Hamblin, as well as the next generation, Helen Borley and Alison Walsh. They are a constant source of inspiration.

Last, but not least, I would like to thank my sons, Sam and Joshua, without whom not only couldn't I have written this book, but there would have been no point.

Sara Alston

Preface

A person with ADHD and a dyslexic walk into a bar. That's literally how we started this journey. One of us was completely distracted and the other made messy notes. We both got sensory overload, gave up and walked away. And so, our journey to writing began. We weren't the usual pair of bespectacled wordsmiths; instead we were a hilarious duo – we promised to enjoy each other's foibles and not let normal expectations haunt us.

Daniel Sobel had already published a couple of successful books and, through his work with thousands of schools, really wanted to cover what he considered to be the most important aspect of inclusion: how to help teachers do it successfully. However, with Daniel's area of expertise being in whole-school management and pastoral leadership, he reached out to his most obvious writing partner, someone he thought was the best person in the world to bring this vision to reality: Sara Alston. Sara was initially anxious about writing a book because of her dyslexia, despite a long career in writing and having written for Daniel's online training courses.

The initial stages were enjoyable as we eagerly swapped ideas about how we could structure this book and what we would want it to say, but we realised there was a long way to go! It's strange to be sitting together now, at the end of this massive journey, writing this final sentence (no, you don't write a book in order!). A person with ADHD and a dyslexic walked into a bar, bought a drink and reflected on the book that they had just written!

The guidance in this book comes from a wealth of first-hand experience, both as teachers and professionals working in primary and secondary education, and also as children with special educational needs. With that in mind, we wanted to begin by each taking the time to introduce ourselves and tell you a little more about why and how we came to be writing this book together.

Sara Alston

Despite, or possibly because of, my dyslexia, I have been teaching for over 30 years in primary schools and special educational needs and disabilities (SEND) units as a class teacher, school leader and designated safeguarding lead. I still work part-time at the 'chalk face' as a special educational needs coordinator (SENCO), as well as working as a successful education consultant and trainer.

Teaching never came easy for me, but it was and is driven by my belief that the child and their welfare are paramount. This must be the starting point for everything that we do as teachers. I was not one of those 'outstanding' teachers because I wouldn't play the game. I believed that being a teacher who cared for and supported their children every day was more important. The children had to come before the Ofsted criteria. This means that when I work with teachers, I know that it is often not easy, and I make a point of never asking teachers to try something that I don't think I could manage myself. It is this, along with my experience of working with children, teachers and support staff, backed by academic research, that I want to share with you in this book.

I have been fortunate in my career to have had the opportunity to extend my experience beyond the classroom. As an advisory teacher, I was involved in the development of resources to support the delivery of the first National Curriculum for history, and more recently through safeguarding and SEND work. This has allowed me to focus on what we do in schools, how it works and how it can be developed.

I first met Daniel in the intimidating surroundings of the Institute of Directors in London and had expected a besuited 'corporate' man. Instead I found an inspiring maverick who cared deeply and passionately about education and supporting teachers to support children. He had taken this vision and built a successful partnership of real experts in his organisation Inclusion Expert, sharing his perception and wisdom as widely as possible. Quickly, I found that Daniel shared much of my personal and professional understanding about the impact of both 'good' and 'bad' experiences of schools on children. Through five years of working together and numerous, at times unlikely and disjointed, conversations, we developed a shared understanding of what it means to support children with SEND in schools. It is also clear to us that the strategies that best support children with special needs in fact support all children to learn better and make teachers' lives more manageable. Our approach is not about major interventions, but about the small tweaks and adaptations that make the difference. This is what we hope to share with you in this book.

Daniel Sobel

Before I write another word in this book, I feel I should confess. Actually, whenever the topic of classroom teaching comes up, I'm very open with everyone that I have never been one of those super-amazing teachers who make it all look easy. I was a firmly 'good' teacher who, when observed, would always get an 'outstanding' for no other reason than I knew when the observation was going to happen and what they were looking for. I was always surprised when someone didn't get an outstanding rating – surely observation is a simple game to win.

Part of the reason I wasn't a consistently 'outstanding' teacher is because I didn't actually agree with a lot of the criteria and had my own thoughts about what teaching could or should be. I'm not promoting rebellion in the ranks! But, as a teacher, I was never going to simply fit in and just do as I was told. I found my way to the back office and school administration as a SENCO, pastoral leader and senior leader, and it was there that I developed my individual approach and invented new ways of doing things.

So, it's clear that I don't profess to be a great teacher. By working with thousands of schools, I have had the privilege to meet some of the best teachers and educators in the country, and have certainly learned a lot along the way, but I could not have written this book on my own. It is for this reason that I partnered with one of the best in the business: Sara Alston. She brings to our duo that genuinely outstanding teachership, as well as vast experience coaching thousands of teachers, and a deeply sophisticated appreciation of how classrooms can work for all in an easier way.

What I bring to the table are a lot of questions and thoughts about teaching and inclusion based on my experiences, which I believe helped to drive our book. We extend a variety of good ideas for all teachers, regardless of age, stage and curriculum, but it is a bit more than that for me. I view this book as a manifesto for a new epoch in the way we approach inclusive thinking.

Introduction

When we set out to write this book about what it means to support children with special educational needs (SEN) in the classroom, our fear was less about what we were going to say and more about what the entire SEN industry has already solidified into the minds of teachers and school leaders. In particular: SEN is expensive; it takes up huge amounts of time; it is the bane of teachers' classes and it can be one of the toughest challenges in parental relationships. Anything we suggest, therefore, has to consider these preconceptions, which is why we have kept the focus of all of our writing on the following principle:

For it to be effective, inclusion has to take up less time, less money and less stress.

Our book is all about how to do inclusive teaching in a stress-free and time-saving way. We look at how to make an 'inclusive classroom' without the pain and effort usually attributed to inclusion. Our focus is on workable tweaks and adaptations that any primary or secondary classroom teacher can use to differentiate for children with SEN. Our whole approach is rooted in a macro idea, which in itself isn't new, but is new in application to efficient SEN and inclusion in the classroom: the phases of the lesson. We break down the lesson into a series of manageable chunks or 'phases'. Inclusion is hard if you think of the lesson as one long marathon with lots of differentiated points along the way for lots of different children. Instead it's easier to think of a lesson as a series of routines and priorities that can become enmeshed in good practice and that can be useful for all children, not just those identified as SEN. By SEN, we include any child who requires additional educational support for cognitive and neurological needs, social and psychological needs, as well as physical and medical needs and so on. This may go significantly beyond the official SEN register.

We know that it's not easy

Teaching children with a range of strengths and needs can be a real challenge. We will be the first to hold up our hands and declare we've got it wrong – we've had days where we felt that we were no good as teachers or that we'd failed to do enough, whether it be in marking or preparation, and so on. There is no such thing as a teacher who gets it consistently right all day, every day without fail, even those declared to be outstanding.

It's funny, though, that we seem to be OK with putting teachers in the firing line to face a group of children when they are woefully untrained and underprepared. There may be some very good reasons for this, but we must confess we can't think of any. Perhaps it is due to the cost of training in both time and money, but we dare say it doesn't cost as much as the sick days of stressed teachers and the teachers who end up leaving the profession in droves (Department for Education, 2020). If you were tasked with a job in a hands-on profession but were not fully prepared for it, HR would view it as negligent, and most likely the line manager would get a rap on the knuckles for insisting you use a piece of machinery you had inadequate training for! We are genuinely worried for the teachers, but the impact that under-trained teachers have on the number of children who are excluded each year is sadly immense. The number of permanent exclusions across all state-funded primary, secondary and special schools has increased from 6,685 in 2015–16 to 7,720 in 2016–17 (Department for Education, 2018). Although we tend to think of it as the 'child's fault', unfortunately it is nearly always our collective failure as teachers and schools when such cases go wrong.

Indeed, one of the most common causes of exclusions is attention deficit hyperactivity disorder (ADHD; UK ADHD Partnership) and those cases usually have something to do with just how (understandably) disruptive the excluded child is for teachers and the normal operation of the school. In those cases, it becomes 'normal' to talk about the child needing another setting – somewhere more specialised where the staff have more or different training. Actually, those special settings, such as a pupil referral unit (PRU), alternative provision (AP) and even social, emotional and mental health (SEMH) provision, are not that dissimilar to the mainstream, and the smaller classes don't make ADHD or other needs disappear. Exactly the same challenges exist in those settings as the mainstream, such as encouraging the child to participate in learning throughout the lesson. Being a specialist setting doesn't give those teachers a magic wand to change the children. Those who do it best are not doing anything different from the outstanding mainstream schools that don't need to exclude students because they have fantastic pedagogy. Pedagogy is the key – how inclusive the teaching is comes down to how skilful the teacher is in understanding and catering for the needs of all children. If you're a school leader, think about how many teachers in your school know how to easily adapt their teaching to meet the needs of a child who bursts into the class and won't settle. If they don't, then is it really fair to ask them to teach that child? If you're a teacher and you feel you haven't had adequate training to cope in these situations, then you've come to the right place. We wish we had had the benefit of the training that is contained in this book. In our view, it is not just 'nice to know stuff'; rather, it should be considered absolutely fundamental to any teaching of mixed groups.

I was about 13 in the mid 1980s, when the craft, design and technology (CDT) teacher set a project for us boys to do over two terms. It was simple: design and build a plane to be launched from a standing position. This is something that the school had done for decades and the school record was something like 20 metres. Most of the boys worked studiously, employing what they had learned about balsa wood and various types of metal work. For me, this was tantamount to a free double period every week.

There was no way that a child with my ADHD could plan and execute a six-month-long project. With just two weeks to go before the showdown (so that's the final four hours), I looked at the fierce competition and admired their varnished wood and fanciful launch contraptions appearing like Iron Age weapons of war. It occurred to me that instead of submitting the absolute zilch that I had failed to produce, I might give this a go, and the easiest and quickest possible thing for me to do would be to make a paper aeroplane. I made the five types every boy in my class knew how to make and worked out which one actually went furthest once and for all. I then tried it with the next paper size up: A3. That worked. I wondered whether it would still work at A2. It did. Each time it went further but the wings got a bit floppy. So, I thought, why not make it in A2 card paper? That sorted out that problem. Hang on, what about an A1 card paper aeroplane? I discovered after one try that with a bit of reinforcing here and there, I had achieved perfection in aviation (why wasn't I working for NASA?). That took one lesson. Now I was into it, I thought about it some more at home. My launch arm was only so long and strong so I figured out that I could use a huge elastic band – but I didn't have one... except in my sports shorts. I quickly cut them open with scissors, pulled out the elastic and took it to school for the next lesson. I made a latch under the plane, reinforced it with a bit more cardboard and double checked it did not alter the aerodynamics. I took the plane outside, put the elastic in the notch and pulled it back like a catapult. I didn't measure it, but it went further than the length of the field, which was at least 50 metres.

The day of the showdown arrived and when I arrived late at the start line, most of the planes had already taken off. Most had flopped, despite looking very sophisticated. My turn. There was only one to beat: his had gone 8.6 metres. I drew back and I remember hearing the surprise of my peers as my plane landed some 70 metres away. For someone who had never achieved anything in CDT and had struggled at school in a myriad of ways, this was a moment for me that I would never forget. I beat the school record by more than three times. One week later, we received the marks for our projects. I was given a D.

Daniel

One of my earliest memories of school, after solving the mystery of why the six Sara(h)s in my class were not listed together in the register (apparently it had something to do with surnames), was spelling tests. The teacher used to point at us and make us spell the words aloud. If we spelled the word wrong, we had to stand up, then stand on the chair if we spelled another word wrong, and then on the desk. Of course, I couldn't spell and certainly couldn't spell out loud. The more I failed to spell the words, the more the teacher pointed at me and demanded I did. I got to the point where I was

> *'lapping' people – standing on the desk for the third or fourth time while they shifted uncomfortably in their seats, witnessing my distress and humiliation at the teacher's bullying. Much of my approach to teaching has been built on a belief that no child should be made to feel as I did then. Equally, no teacher should be so inadequately prepared for teaching that they feel this is an appropriate way to behave.*
>
> *Sara*

To label or not to label?

We are the beneficiaries of diagnosis being more recognised and available. At school we were both labelled as 'lazy' and 'thick'. Now, every teacher in the country knows what ADHD and dyslexia are, at least in principle. So, when it comes to labels, let's not throw the baby out with the bathwater. It is common for people with SEN to gain some relief from finally knowing what is up with them.

> *For me, receiving my diagnosis of dyslexia at the age of 11 gave me an explanation as to why I found learning so difficult. For my whole primary school career, I was told that I was 'thick' or 'lazy' or both. At some level, I had always felt that it was not true but could think of no other explanation of why I found reading and writing so difficult. I was given a 'word' – dyslexia – that explained my experience and enabled me to find the courage to go on.*
>
> *Sara*

It seems we humans need labels. We are reminded of the idea in Yuval Noah Harari's *Sapiens: A Brief History of Humankind* (2014) that our human brains developed on the plains in Africa where we learned to recognise patterns and give names to things. This ingenuity has driven humankind's development. We would not know about ADHD without recognising the pattern. Our teachers would not know about ADHD without it being normal to label, and for that label to mean there is an identifiable pattern. Teachers and children experienced ADHD before the label existed. They recognised and experienced the behaviours associated with ADHD, but they were dismissed as naughty, delinquent, disturbed and so on. As the language of special needs has moved, in less than 70 years, from 'educationally subnormal' to 'retarded' to 'special needs', we have developed the ability to look at these patterns of behaviour and change the perception of them as 'different' and 'wrong' to something we can identify, describe and ultimately support.

However, the labels remain too broad. They tell us about the general, not the specific. There are about 10,500 species and a further 21,000 subspecies under the label of 'bird', a term that is not so helpful for differentiating between a chicken and an eagle. Similarly, 'ADHD' gives us general information, but does not identify the detail about the individual.

There are endless academic arguments over labelling. Pro-labellers insist that labelling children gives their teachers the necessary information to treat them appropriately and provide academic accommodations for them. Anti-labellers protest not only that labelling children will exclude them socially, but also that labels are associated with stigma and stereotypes, which prejudice teachers against students with SEN (Cheng). There are many parents and indeed children whom we have both worked with who have appreciated being able to give a name to their challenges, especially because it can validate them being 'normal for someone with condition X'. Equally, we have seen a label become a crutch and an excuse for lack of aspiration. Too many times we have heard a parent say, 'I just want my child to fit in and be happy' and so avoid any focus on their learning. The biggest problem we have borne witness to is how teachers can (very understandably) see the child through the prism of a diagnosis that they have read in a formal assessment or medical document as opposed to how that condition may manifest itself with each individual in their classroom. It's not that the diagnosis is wrong – this is beyond our scope as educators. It's that it is, by definition, a limited understanding: it is just the diagnosis – it is not a commentary on the child's biography, personality and moods. It doesn't account for the machinations and dramas of friendships and relationships, the intricacy and pervading undercurrents of big-themed fears and overly passionate obsessions. All these nuances form the real picture of the child and go far beyond a medicalised or diagnostic view of a whole being. It is precisely these broader issues that will influence the child's participation in our classrooms and will be the most useful and practical knowledge for maximising engagement. In a way, the diagnosis can be as much a hindrance as it is a help to seeing the real child. The majority of mainstream teachers are aware of commonly found challenges such as autism, dyslexia and other medical-sounding names. However, we have failed to educate our teachers in how these terms are spectrums and are not fixed conditions where all children with them will appear the same. As a result, the label can actually end up obscuring the individual's real needs.

In 1996, Fox and Stinnett concluded that using the then-accepted phrase 'seriously emotionally disturbed' as a label would elicit a bias against the individual, both in the present and in the future. Today, we take it for granted that this is true, but it took some evolution of human thought and society to reach this understanding. Moving forward to a 2018 study by a team based in Japan (Kayama and Haight), and they take this to a whole new level: any label leads to some type of social isolation. They also found that many parents preferred school support to be holistic and unobtrusive rather than aimed in a pinpoint fashion at their child. A European version of this study published by the European Agency for Development in Special Needs Education back in 2009 found that it was mostly the parents who were wary of any labelling stigma rather than the children. Perhaps this is a generational and cultural issue?

Willis (2014) built on something that we know to be a far bigger issue than we admit to among teachers: that we prejudge students. She emphasised that this is more pronounced when students are labelled with a SEN that implies behaviour challenges or emotional problems, arguing that teachers are often scared of these children. The main difficulties teachers have with inclusion in general seems to be 'maintaining discipline' and approaching emotional or behavioural disorder (EBD) children appropriately. We know that, as a profession, teachers are not against inclusion, but many feel that they have not received adequate training, and most importantly this leaves many teachers feeling ill-equipped and unable to deal with the behaviours frequently associated with SEN.

The group that students find themselves placed in often reinforces an opinion that others may have about them. This is typically seen in larger classroom sets. Teachers, indeed schools in general, regularly organise children to work in groups according to ability, which often reflect deeper divisions within cohorts of children. In her book, *Some Kids I Taught and What They Taught Me* (2019), the poet and teacher Kate Clanchy describes the disillusionment and anger of 'Set 3' whom no one wanted to teach; due to a combination of learning, behavioural and social difficulties, 'Set 3' were unable to access the curriculum, but lacked the support given to 'Set 4' to overcome these issues. In schools and classrooms, the focus of support is commonly given to those with SEN, or others who meet the criteria for inclusion in a vulnerable group, but those who are just above the threshold are left to flounder and fail.

It seems therefore that the research is generally pointing in the direction of labels not being helpful in today's world. We, along with our colleagues at Inclusion Expert, tend to agree with this and have developed a bias against labelling because, as practitioners, we have seen from our work in thousands of schools that there are many problems with labelling. These include:

- Many children are given a diagnosis, which is then seen as the answer to all their difficulties. But a diagnosis does not tell the teacher how to support the child. The diagnosis can act as a signpost, but it does not provide the detail of the support and adjustments the child needs to learn and be happy in school.

- Confusingly, many children are given the same diagnosis, but present with different needs in the classroom, while children with different diagnoses present with similar needs.

- Teachers need support and confidence to move beyond the label and see the whole child, including their strengths and their barriers to learning, so that they are best able to support them.

We do not seek to rebel against the medical world; this is not our expertise. Equally, education is not the expertise of most medical professionals. It is a matter of identifying what information is relevant to teachers and how best to use it to support children.

A diagnosis of autism spectrum disorder (ASD), or any other difficulty, does not necessarily make a difference to a child's needs in the classroom. Hopefully, most teachers will have begun to put support in place for the child long before a label is given.

> *I remember being completely set up for exam revision. Not only did I have all the books and notes I needed (photocopied from a kind friend), but I had the beverages and snacks, perfect lighting and quiet space, and even the questions from previous papers so I knew exactly what they were going to ask. Yet, when I looked at the first page, my eyes couldn't concentrate. I remember looking at it for the best part of an hour and making no progress at all. The important aspect to take from this reflection is not the challenge to get my mind to concentrate, but what it did to me psychologically to feel like such a failure. I'm not Einstein now, but I'm a published author with a number of postgrads under my belt and a confidence from those around me who respect my thinking and consider me 'bright'. This is completely at odds with the way I perceived myself as a teenager. The result was me having the 'self-esteem of an ant', as a therapist friend once put it to me, and an absolute belief that I was truly never going to get anywhere, which was coupled with quite an inquisitive and sharp mind. This last bit leaked out as arrogance in my early adulthood – my self-perception was inconsistent with the way I presented myself to others.*
>
> *Daniel*

One example of the different 'types' of SEN shows this principle in action. Each of these students has an ASD diagnosis but presents in different ways to the teacher in the classroom:

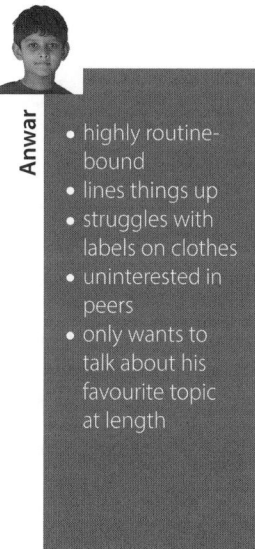

Anwar

- highly routine-bound
- lines things up
- struggles with labels on clothes
- uninterested in peers
- only wants to talk about his favourite topic at length

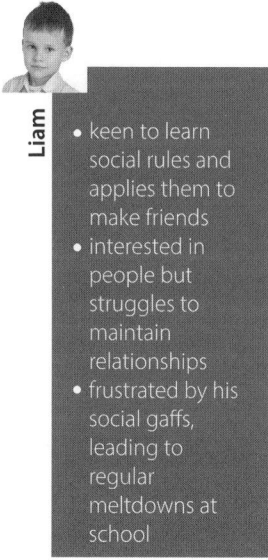

Liam

- keen to learn social rules and applies them to make friends
- interested in people but struggles to maintain relationships
- frustrated by his social gaffs, leading to regular meltdowns at school

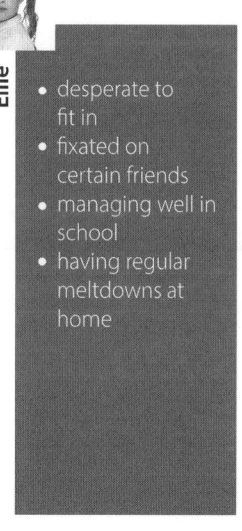

Ellie

- desperate to fit in
- fixated on certain friends
- managing well in school
- having regular meltdowns at home

Similarly, consider three students who all have different diagnoses of dyslexia, ADHD and ASD but who present with the same challenges in the classroom:

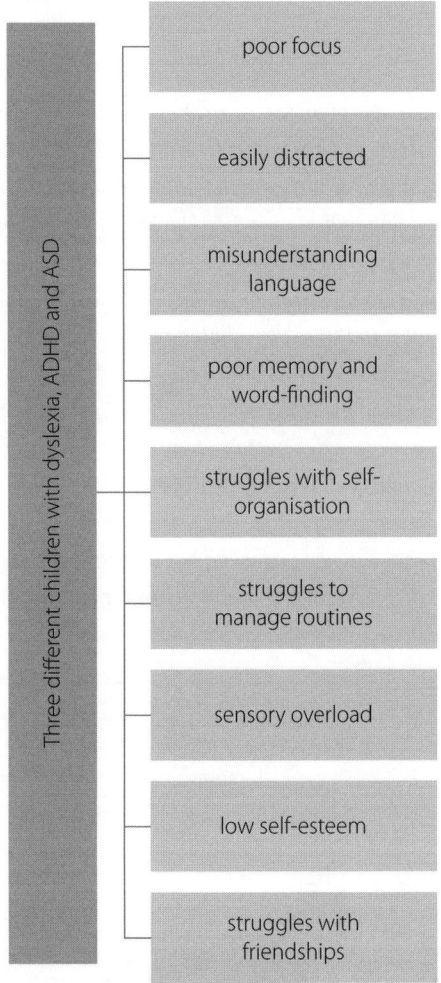

Three different children with dyslexia, ADHD and ASD

- poor focus
- easily distracted
- misunderstanding language
- poor memory and word-finding
- struggles with self-organisation
- struggles to manage routines
- sensory overload
- low self-esteem
- struggles with friendships

Case study: A post-adoption meeting

In a post-adoption meeting with a parent whose child had hit crisis point, the various professionals were using up the very limited time discussing whether the child met the criteria for diagnosis of attachment issues, ADHD, foetal alcohol syndrome difficulties or sensory processing difficulties. The discussion was going nowhere, and the meeting was about to end with no change for the child. However, by changing the focus to identifying the child's needs and finding ways to support them, the team could finally make progress to help the child simply get on. This is an example of a child with a range of complex needs from a collection of co-occurring diagnoses. The challenge for the class teacher is to meet those needs so that they and others in their class can learn. We need to start with the child and their needs, not the diagnosis.

Moving beyond labels

We believe that two fundamental actions are needed in SEN practice in order for teachers to progress from the old way of thinking about diagnosis:

1. understanding that SEN encompasses strengths as well as difficulties
2. looking beyond diagnosis to determine *how* to support each individual child.

Let's consider each of these in turn.

Understanding that SEN encompasses strengths and difficulties

First and foremost, we need to change the deficit model of SEN to one that encompasses strengths as well as difficulties, leading to a more personalised approach. The most common question for teachers when told a child in their new class has SEN is: 'What do they find difficult?' Even as a SENCO, when told a child with SEN is joining the school, our first questions tend to focus on the ways they demonstrate their SEN and the support they need. We rarely ask about their strengths and motivations.

Different people display their special needs in different ways, and there are strengths that come with most non-neurotypical development. Views of SEN are often polarised. For example, popular views of autism include the antisocial geniuses, such as Alan Turing, or the *Rain Man*-type savant, or the locked-in non-verbal 'head banger'. The extremes of autism stereotypes were reflected in the work of the early pioneers in the development of autism. Asperger had his 'little professors' and focused on their abilities, while Kanner focused on 'locked-in' children and blamed 'toxic parenting' (Silberman, 2015). For most people with autism, the truth is somewhere in between. We need to avoid developing a 'special need as superpower' view and see children as whole people with strengths and difficulties, not just a descriptor of need.

It is interesting to see what advantages teachers perceive children with SEN as having. The table on page 10 gives some examples.

Dyslexia	ADHD	Autism
• visual thinking • creative and interconnected thinking • navigation • big-picture thinking • pattern recognition: useful for prediction • spatial knowledge • sharper peripheral vision • narrative reasoning • verbal communication • good at reading people	• curious • highly engaged in the moment • energetic • creative • persistent • adventurous • big-picture thinking • thinking outside the box • copes well with unpredictability	• attention to detail and observational skills • logical • long-term memory and recall of details • unswayed by peer pressure • reliable, loyal, honest • non-judgemental • knowledge of routines and desire for accuracy and order • ability to hyper-focus • thinking outside the box • visual learning • good vocabulary (though they do not always understand the words they use)

Case study: Paul

Paul is a Year 3 boy with an education, health and care plan (EHCP) and an ASD diagnosis who suffers significant social anxiety. He has a near-photographic memory, which means that his knowledge and recall, if not actual understanding, of rote learning such as spelling and times tables is brilliant. Recently, Paul was supported to enter a whole-school spelling bee and was runner-up. After a detailed run-through of what would happen, supported by visuals and keeping his trusted class teacher in sight for support, Paul stood up in front of the whole school and answered the questions. The belief and recognition of this specific strength, supported by specific strategies, gave Paul the confidence and motivation to manage his anxiety and to succeed, building his confidence for the future.

It is important to remember that different people show different strengths, and co-occurring diagnoses produce different and unique combinations of strengths and difficulties. There are many examples of famous people with different diagnoses that can be useful as illustrative examples of this: Albert Einstein is variously identified as having ADHD, ASD and dyslexia, while Richard Branson has been diagnosed with ADHD and dyslexia. What is clear is that each diagnosis comes with both strengths and difficulties. This has led to a situation where there appears to be a growing 'cult' of famous dyslexics, and at times it can feel as though the diagnosis has almost become a status symbol. This can add to parental demand for diagnosis, in addition to the pressure created by diagnosis via internet research.

Looking beyond diagnosis

When a child is given a diagnosis, this does not tell the teacher (or parents) *how* to include the child effectively in the classroom, though it can act as an indicator of which direction to look in for the best support for the child.

Case study: Mohammed

Mohammed was given a diagnosis of ASD and ADHD by Child and Adolescent Mental Health Services (CAMHS) and, with the agreement of his parents, was medicated. He received appointments to monitor the medication, but there was no support for the school or, even more importantly in this case, his parents about how to manage him and his behaviour. Nothing in his behaviour was changed by the diagnosis. He continued to be rude to people without understanding that he had been rude or what this meant. The school was left with the task of supporting both Mohammed and his parents based on his needs, with the added challenge of managing his parents' feelings of anger and disappointment that the diagnosis did not change their child.

The problem is exacerbated by the fact that the diagnosticians often come from a health service. They consider the evidence and make a diagnosis. If that requires medical intervention, they act. However, when it does not, as in many cases of ASD and ADHD, they take no further action.

Regardless of a diagnosis or not, hopefully most teachers will have begun to put support in place for the child, long before an assessment is made, in response to the needs the child exhibits. The diagnosis itself does not change what the child needs; it merely confirms and adds information to support the approaches being used. Putting this into practice is the expertise of the teacher.

However, this is an area where many teachers feel that they lack the necessary expertise, and rightly so considering how little time SEN is usually given at initial teacher training. Often, there are a lot of feelings of frustration and upset on behalf of the teacher to not be able to include this child effectively. Therefore, there is way too much misplaced hope that once a diagnosis is made for a child, the teacher will finally be given everything they need to solve the problem of how to have this child in their class and suddenly the learning will be easier for the child. The diagnosis is seen as a magic answer, but in reality, it never is. At best, it is a confirmation of what we already suspected.

We understand that for many parents and some professionals there is a belief or hope that from a diagnosis will grow the cure – that if the child has a diagnosis, somehow this will solve or excuse any difficulties. For some, it may excuse inaction as they feel 'there is nothing that can be done', so there is no need to try to improve conditions for the child or promote their learning.

There are only three reasons for a school to support seeking a diagnosis for a child:

- to access funding
- to give staff direction in understanding and helping a child and their needs because this is not known, despite their efforts
- to support the child's self-esteem by providing an explanation of their difficulties that they themselves can understand, or to support the parents to understand that there are issues with their child beyond their parenting.

Yet in reality, diagnoses are sought for a wide range of other reasons of varying legitimacy, which can impact on the support the child receives and more importantly how the child is perceived and perceives themselves.

Labels get resources

There is a problem that most classroom teachers might not be aware of but SENCOs and school leaders live with on a daily basis. In our current approach, there is a tension between labelling the child and getting resources for them, and allowing the child to be punished for behaviours and otherwise labelled – meaning either you say they have special needs, give them all the help they need and don't take normal punitive action *or* you say they are just badly behaved and let the full force of behavioural policies be implemented. We think that this is a false dichotomy.

Labels create excuses

In 2019, Maras et al. did a brilliant piece of research exploring this. A mock court was set up, and jury-eligible participants were given a description of a male who had been taken in for suspicious and aggressive behaviours; half the 'jury' were also informed that he had autism spectrum disorder and were given background information on autism, while the other half only received the basic description. The participants in the 'label' group attributed the defendant's behaviours to autism, were more likely to give either a not guilty verdict or more lenient sentencing and described the defendant as honest and likeable. The opposite was true for the 'no label' group. Like the 'jurors', teachers may tolerate behaviours or have lower expectations of students with a label.

In reality, by labelling the child you create an alternative level of problem of perception for both children and teachers. Our biggest worry about labels was articulated in a 2014 study by Staples-Farmer, which demonstrates the sad truth that labels actually form part of a child's identity. Once labelled, children are likely to aspire to the label and nothing more. The study went on to show that for juvenile offenders, there is some evidence that reducing or eradicating labels can help them to reconstruct and change their identities with higher aspirations. Further, in 2014, Iudici et al. found that children with label diagnoses will attribute their successes to their medication, and their failures to their inability to 'erase' their label. Parents see this as equivalent to the 'cause' of their child's behaviour. By using diagnoses in this way, 'labelled children' can justify any behaviour in the classroom and children are reduced to their label and not seen as a whole person with a range of needs and strengths.

Labels create awareness, but of what?
In 2001, Campbell et al. sampled a group of teachers planning for meeting the needs of students with SEN without providing labels for the types of SEN. Instead the teachers were given detailed, nuanced information about the students' individual presenting needs. This led to a significant increase in staff using strength-based approaches, including no labels for the child.

Further, McMahon (2012) showed that trainee teachers appear to believe that there are two types of labelling:

1. a teacher's amateur diagnosis of children's disruptive and repeated behaviours as ADHD
2. a medical diagnosis of ADHD, which causes teachers to label the students as 'disengaged' or 'difficult', and so to choose not to put extra effort into the child's education.

So, school-based labelling was considered negative, whereas medical diagnoses were considered positive, but placed a limit on the expectations had of the child.

Emotional meaning of a label
Ohan et al. (2011) discussed identical studies of teachers and children where half of the children had descriptions labelling them with ADHD. Teachers were more willing to provide support to other professionals to help the children with an ADHD label, but reacted to the ADHD-labelled individuals with more negative emotions. The conclusion they came to is, in our view, the most significant point: teachers with substantial training in ADHD were emotionally influenced by the labels but rated their willingness to help all children (with or without label) more equally.

Belonging and identity

Roger Slee (2019) makes a point that is hidden in plain sight: that most schools, including their academic and social structures, were created before (and without regard to) the needs or requirements of 'other' groups (including SEN students). Thus, schools that are built from the ground up as 'owning and valuing' all children are more inclusive. Feelings of 'belonging' are currently popular in educational research and are tightly connected to definitions of identity. That is, how someone identifies themselves determines their sense of belonging to a group. A lot of this research is gender-related, but applicable to SEN nonetheless. A sense of belonging seems to be based on external acknowledgment and acceptance, as well as a conscious effort by the individual to 'look' like everyone else. Belonging, like identity, has two sides: the individual's perception of themselves and others' perceptions of them. A deep-seated sense of belonging is rooted in both of these perceptions being in alignment.

Barriers to belonging

We are sceptical about much of the excitement around Finnish education. However, a piece of useful research from 2016 (Pesonen et al.) attempted to describe some of the barriers to 'belonging' for students with SEN, including:

- teachers not respecting the children's individual needs and treating or teaching them accordingly
- being victimised and/or rejected by their peers
- stigma associated with their diagnostic label.

So, what helped with 'belonging'? Unsurprisingly, close relationships with adults at school, being treated with respect by those adults, and appropriate accommodations being made without judgement for their special needs.

Mahar et al. (2013) tell us that 'belonging' may seem to be a 'wishy washy' word as it is a particularly subjective value. We can, however, state that it is rooted in external relationships that treat the individual with respect and give them value. It is precisely this external relationship that seems to be important. It must be with an authority member of the group to which the individual wants to belong, in this case the teacher.

SEN and SEND as an identity

Evan Odell's (2019) report for Disability Rights UK on 'Young people's attitudes to disability' found that few of the pupils with SEND identified themselves as disabled. The majority of the children surveyed defined disability by the use of aids, particularly wheelchairs. The pupils with SEND who received extra support or reasonable adjustments were not sure why they received them or what they were for. Also, pupils with SEND were described as being more bullied, socially excluded and having fewer friends. Both the SEND and non-SEND pupils expressed neutral to positive attitudes to disabled children but did not identify themselves as being friends with them.

Case study: Robin

Robin has ASD traits and was referred to CAMHS, but while he was on the waiting list his newborn brother died. As a result, CAMHS explained that they couldn't see him as it had now become a bereavement issue, and they referred him to a local child bereavement counselling charity. However, the bereavement charity explained that they couldn't see him as his problems were beyond bereavement. Meanwhile, the child and family received no support.

A recognition of this problem is reflected in the current move in safeguarding work to develop a single pathway to protect and support children who may be affected by a range of related issues: criminal and sexual exploitation, county lines, serious violence, gang involvement, human trafficking and modern-day slavery. Historically, children were channelled into separate support pathways for each issue, but we now know that they are frequently interlinked and co-occurring. To support children effectively, we need to focus on their needs rather than dividing the exploitation they are experiencing into subsets. Similarly, in supporting children with SEN, we need to consider the whole child and their needs, not divide our pathways of support according to a label.

Inclusion is a language

Part of the process of changing the way teachers regard SEN is to encourage them to consider the language they use to describe children in general, and those with SEN in particular. We need to reframe our language to reflect a focus on the child's needs. By understanding children's needs and how they are demonstrated in behaviours, we can see that a child might be *in* distress rather than simply see them as *causing* distress. This can reduce the teacher's stress and resentment of what they may feel to be a wilful disturbance of their class. Supporting teachers to have a more optimistic and understanding approach can help to prevent many of the secondary problems that co-occur with SEN children, such as poor self-esteem and a lack of confidence to engage and participate meaningfully.

Labels can obscure the bespoke approach

By focusing on the child's needs, strengths and motivators, we can provide more individualised, focused and consequently effective support for their learning. An over-emphasis on 'labels' can inhibit this and obscure the child from view.

So, why do we care so much about the labels?

We've tried to include a full account of the academic basis of our thinking around labels to buttress our personal experiences. We appreciate this is an ongoing debate and so we have tried to lay out what we think are the most convincing series of points that all educators could consider. The important part for us and for this book is to see each child as an individual and not as a set of assumptions based on what their 'labels' tell you they are like.

When our starting points are 'individuals', we are more able to make subtle adaptations and tweaks to support them. This book is all about how to implement those tweaks and adaptations really simply and effectively. As we will say many times, these adaptations are good for many children and can be happily renamed 'good inclusive teaching'. This differs from the broadly accepted model that you have a child with a diagnosis of SEN and therefore you should adhere to the differentiation models laid out in the professional guidance related to their particular diagnosis. These differentiations are often sweeping, generalised catch-alls and thus ineffective.

Case study: Parents seeking diagnoses of dyslexia

A number of parents from a school had sought diagnoses of dyslexia for their children from a local expert. While the assessment data varied to reflect the children's strengths and difficulties, the expert's recommendations showed little variation. All the reports recommended the same level of support, the same provisions and the same strategies, regardless of the child's level of need or specific difficulties. The strategies were a response to the label and not the needs of the child. This one-size-fits-all approach left the school trying to explain to the parents why they were not following the advice. The school's approach was based on the needs of the child and a recognition that not all children with a diagnosis of dyslexia needed or were supported by the same strategies. This led to a number of difficult conversations.

Indeed, we have found a common disgruntlement among SENCOs and inclusion leads across the UK and in various other countries where we have trained staff that the advice from many diagnosing experts tends to be too generic. The lack of clarity means that there is often a gap between the diagnostic guidance and the reality of the child in the classroom, which causes frustrations for teachers, parents and, most importantly, the child. We have said above that there are benefits to diagnosis and we are not in any way arguing against the medical or psychology professionals. The key point is how these diagnoses are used specifically in the context of education.

Inclusion is mainly just good teaching

'I wish I could persuade everyone that most of what teaching children with additional needs involves is simply good teaching.' Daniel Sobel

Before we begin this book in earnest, we feel it's important to acknowledge that at the heart of the inclusive classroom is simply good teaching. There's no magic to good teaching; it's mostly 'tricks'. The best 'tricks' we have to offer are not particularly special and unusual; they don't give birth to wry smiles and pensive holdings of the chin. The most inclusive teachers we have seen are really just focused on good teaching. But what does this mean? You probably don't need our book to lay this out for the first time – we would be surprised if this is the very first book on teaching you have ever come across! This section is therefore going to emphasise what you probably already know, so you can use it as a prompt and as a framework to discover that you already know a lot about inclusion and are already doing a huge amount of it.

The obvious but crucial elements of good teaching

Here's a list of what we think are the fairly obvious elements of good teaching that are crucial to get right.

1. Relationships

a) With the children

Fundamental to successful teaching is building relationships and getting to know your children. If you want your children to trust you, particularly those who have been let down or abused in the past, you need to work on building relationships with them. Children need trusted, familiar adults and advocates. Being their class teacher or tutor doesn't give you an immediate entitlement to that trust. Respect is earned. Children know if people don't like them. Key to this is how you talk to and about your children. Language matters: it frames and reveals our thinking. To be a successful teacher and build relationships, we need to consider the impact of our language. This includes not being afraid to admit mistakes and being humble enough to say sorry when we get things wrong.

b) With parents

For many parents, particularly those who did not have good school experiences themselves, engaging with school is difficult. They might not turn up to formal events. They may appear aggressive or defensive. We need to think about what this behaviour is communicating and hiding. To build parents' trust, we need to ensure that we are sharing good news as well as bad. We need to think about how we communicate and the language we use. Is it language that the parents understand? It is so easy as a teacher to slip into jargon. It is our everyday, so we forget it is not everyone else's normal. We need particularly to think about how we communicate about attainment and progress. How do we make this understandable and find positives in a pass-or-fail system for children who year on year are not making age expectations?

We must remember and respect parents' expertise on their child. We might be the education and subject experts, but the parents know their child better than we ever will. We may not agree with them. Children (and adults) present differently in different settings, so what the parents see and experience of their child may be different to what we see, but we need to value their view. It is always worth considering a home visit. This is enlightening in many ways.

c) With other staff in our classroom
Some of us are lucky enough to share our classrooms with teaching assistants (TAs) or learning support assistants (LSAs). The job titles vary, but you know who we mean. There are books written about successfully working with TAs. Suffice to say here, the more you communicate effectively with your teaching assistant (TA) about children and the learning, the greater their impact will be. None of us work well when we are 'winging it', but too often this is what we expect of TAs. They cannot be effective support for and explainers of learning that they are only picking up at the same time as the child. They need to know what we are teaching and why. Further, we need to listen to and value their feedback on what the children have learned.

2. Recognition that some of these things take time

Getting things right takes time, so prepare as much as you can at the beginning of the year. The best way of solving many of the problems that children with additional needs appear to present with is to work preventively before things become an issue, rather than responding reactively to behaviour problems. In reality, this takes extra time, effort, and physical and emotional energy. But it is a case of investing time to save time and energy. Building effective differentiation into each phase of the lesson supports the next stage of the learning.

3. Importance of the use of visuals

The more we can make visual in our classroom, the more it reinforces and helps deliver the key messages and instructions to the children. The easier we make this for us and the children, the more energy they are able to use to learn. So:

- Make your visuals clear and relevant, including for repeated instructions.
- Use pictures to pre-warn of a new activity or changes of lesson pace, such as a video camera to indicate that a film is coming up or a table to show that the children are going to move to their tables.
- Use visuals to support new or technical vocabulary and go on using them to support children with memory or language difficulties.
- Make use of as many 'aide memoires' for your children as possible – mnemonics, rhymes, pictures, actions or whatever will work for the group or individual to support them to embed and take ownership of the learning.

- Make your displays relevant and useful and teach children to use them.

- Consider the impact of an over-stimulating classroom. Try to have a plain wall that some children can face for focused work so they will not be distracted by displays.

Case study: Nur

In a maths assessment, Nur was sitting and staring at the wall and then using her finger to count up and down. It turned out she was visualising the display of a thermometer that had been on the wall until it was taken down for the test, and using it to solve a question about negative numbers.

---

4. Support for struggling readers and the impact of difficulties with reading across the curriculum

Think about support for poor readers across the curriculum. As Mark Seidenberg (2017 page 130) reminds us, 'Children who struggle when reading texts aloud do not become good readers if left to read silently; their dysfluency merely becomes inaudible.' If children cannot or are struggling to access the written language of the classroom, they will struggle to access all the learning. We need to think about the strategies we use to support these children across the curriculum. Too often we ignore their difficulties in lessons that are not focused on language development, so they are supported in English, but not in history or maths. Yet their reading difficulties remain a barrier to learning in those subjects too.

The support we provide for other areas of difficulties often depends on the children using their poor reading skills to access the support. For example, a child who is poor at spelling is given a word bank to help them, ignoring the fact that they can't read the word bank to find the words. We need to think creatively, adding pictures or other visual prompts to help the child find the words or using colours to help separate verbs, nouns and so on.

As a poor speller, I was constantly told to use a dictionary. But as a non-phonological dyslexic, I had no way of finding a word I couldn't spell in a dictionary because I couldn't work out what letters it began with. However, as I had a good vocabulary, I could use a thesaurus to look for a word with a similar meaning that I could spell and then find the word I wanted.

Sara

We need to build our awareness of children's strengths and use these in the support we offer them, rather than expect them to depend on their weak skills to support their other areas of difficulties.

5. Cumulative impact of events across the day or week

We talk throughout the book about the phases of the lesson and the importance of seeing them as part of the child's journey through the day. We can work to support children within our own lesson, but we need to be aware of what else has happened outside of this. Teachers understand the impact of high wind, wet play or a 'wear your own clothes day', but we often miss the impact of the balance of quiet and noisier learning times. Three high-stress lessons on the trot with different people in each lesson, or PE and a noisy lunch break, are going to leave a child less able to calm and self-regulate. Particularly at secondary school, not all the children in the lesson will have had the same lessons before coming to you and so we need to respond to their different experiences. We need to work to use quiet times to support focus and concentration and allow children to calm. This may mean that a child needs time out or calm time before they are ready and able to access learning.

We also need to consider the noise and movement within the class, so we balance quiet learning time against active and noisy learning. We need to balance the need for silent working against the need for self-talk to support emotional regulation and learning.

Further, at the risk of being killjoys, this may include thinking about 'fun' in school. Teachers often confuse what they think is fun or enjoying themselves with what children actually enjoy. In secondary schools, where each teacher is planning their own 'fun', there is a danger of missing the cumulative impact on children. Particularly at the ends of terms, when children are trying to manage transitions with all their implications, we introduce exciting, non-routine, 'fun' activities. This unpredictability increases anxiety and makes life even more difficult to cope with for many children. 'Fun' times can be supported by:

- Sharing the timetable for the period of unpredictability, for example, Christmas preparation and play rehearsals, including using an 'oops card' when there are changes in that timetable (see page 53).

- Ensuring that high-energy, high-stress or high-excitement activities are interspersed with quiet, routine activities. Some children may actually welcome a 'normal' maths lesson as a break from the Christmas madness.

- Considering opt-outs and quiet spaces.

6. Teaching skills that we take for granted

There are many skills that children need to learn successfully, including visualisation, listening and reading for understanding, not just decoding, note-taking, and so on. We tend to take these skills for granted, but children need to have been taught them explicitly. We are often happy to spend time teaching routines, such as lining up or sticking work in straight. Yet, we are less willing to justify to ourselves time spent on skills needed for learning. Time spent teaching these things is almost always time well spent.

Case study: Joshua

Joshua's history teacher picked up his history book and shook it so all the work that he had not stuck in, which was basically all the work he had done in the year, fell onto the floor in front of the whole class. It took six or seven minutes of class time to pick up. He could access the learning but really struggled with the filing skills, which were never taught or supported.

7. Avoid public telling off and consider use of praise

We are often told to 'catch children being good' and most of us try to do this. But we need to be aware of the impact of our praise. Praise needs to be specific, so that the child knows what they are being praised for and why. It also needs to be genuine and not delivered in a way a child can perceive as patronising.

Case study: Samara

Samara had a diagnosis of dyspraxia and struggled with self-organisation. Her teacher wanted to support Samara's self-esteem, which was poor, so she praised her for turning up with all her belongings. Samara felt that she was being praised for doing what was expected of everyone and meeting the bare minimum requirements. She wanted to be praised on the same terms as others and not 'patronised' because she had SEN.

Equally, we need to be aware of the impact of public telling off. It makes children feel embarrassed, angry and ashamed. For some children, this will act as an incentive not to repeat the offence. However, for many it will build resentment and humiliation, which they will communicate through acting out – disruption, aggression, being the 'class clown' or withdrawal. We need to remember that by shouting at children we can be forcing them to relive abuse or distress that we don't know about. It is almost always more effective to speak to a child privately.

It is vital that we are not telling children off for things that they can't help. We should not tell off children with SEN for issues related to their SEN, for example the need to fidget or poor organisation. Further, we should not penalise children for not having resources their parents cannot afford to provide.

8. Metacognition

Metacognition has been the focus of much educational research and debate over recent years, including work from the Education Endowment Foundation (EEF), who rated it as the intervention with the greatest impact and representing the best value for money (2018). It is key for children to develop an understanding of and a vocabulary to describe how they learn. By making the unconscious process of learning conscious and explicit, we can support children to understand how they learn, so they are able to develop strategies to support their learning. As adults, we go through this process when we learn new skills or try to solve a problem. For example:

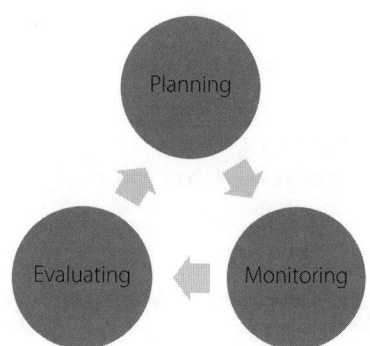

Planning: What am I doing?

- What do I know about problems like this?
- How have I solved them before?
- What resources do I need and where can I find them?

Monitoring: How am I doing?

- What am I finding challenging?
- What do I need to change or edit?
- Do I need additional help?
- How can I help myself?

Evaluating: How did I do?

- What could I do differently next time?
- What other strategies or approaches could I use?
- How will I remember what I have learned?

Developing a culture of differentiation

At the root of our approach to inclusion is the importance of developing a culture of differentiation that impacts the whole class, not just those identified as vulnerable or having SEN. It is about adapting support to meet children's needs and recognising that these needs change, so children may need different support at different times.

Differentiation was the subject of a protracted professional debate within the Inclusion Expert team, which was led by our colleague Wendy Knott. We concluded that the key aspects in creating a 'culture of differentiation' involved eight main elements, the eight Rs:

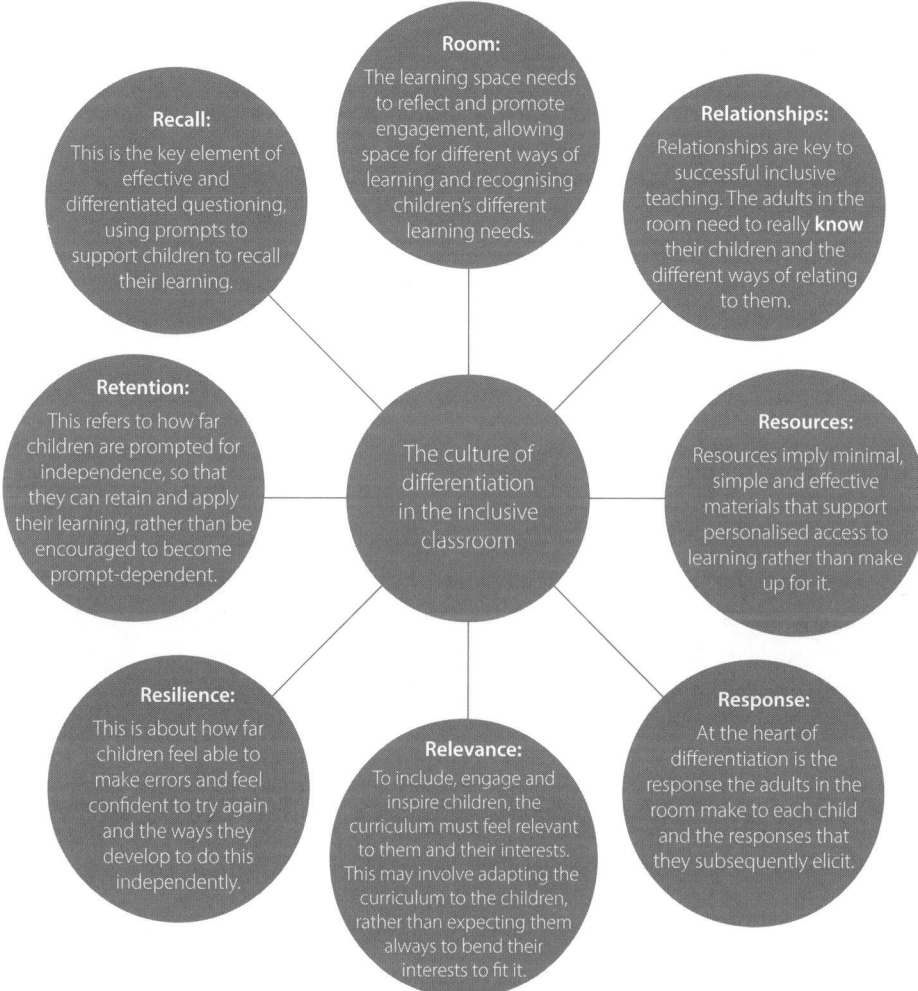

Room:
The learning space needs to reflect and promote engagement, allowing space for different ways of learning and recognising children's different learning needs.

Recall:
This is the key element of effective and differentiated questioning, using prompts to support children to recall their learning.

Relationships:
Relationships are key to successful inclusive teaching. The adults in the room need to really **know** their children and the different ways of relating to them.

Retention:
This refers to how far children are prompted for independence, so that they can retain and apply their learning, rather than be encouraged to become prompt-dependent.

Resources:
Resources imply minimal, simple and effective materials that support personalised access to learning rather than make up for it.

The culture of differentiation in the inclusive classroom

Resilience:
This is about how far children feel able to make errors and feel confident to try again and the ways they develop to do this independently.

Relevance:
To include, engage and inspire children, the curriculum must feel relevant to them and their interests. This may involve adapting the curriculum to the children, rather than expecting them always to bend their interests to fit it.

Response:
At the heart of differentiation is the response the adults in the room make to each child and the responses that they subsequently elicit.

Differentiation is not something that happens at a particular point in the lesson or when children use specific materials. As our culture of differentiation model shows, it permeates the whole lesson. Essentially, it asks how the child is feeling and engaging, how they are being supported, and how independent they feel comfortable being. No worksheet can ever produce the indicators of real learning and belonging that can be developed through an inclusive classroom culture that promotes the attitude, approach and small things that make the biggest difference to a child who is desperate to feel included.

The inclusive classroom engages all children by providing small tweaks to support their learning and engagement.

Case study: Jamie

Thirteen-year-old Jamie is a high-functioning but typical child with Down's syndrome and co-occurring hearing impairment and speech, language and communication difficulties. The eight Rs help him in the following ways:

- **Room:** Jamie has a predictable place in the classroom that is good for his hearing and for social inclusion. He sits with a supportive friend.

- **Relationships:** All staff, both in and out of the classroom, know Jamie. Not only do they understand his needs and barriers to learning, but they also know his strengths and motivations. They have been shown how to communicate with him effectively.

- **Resources:** Jamie has a lesson planner with visual prompts and resources that he uses in every lesson.

- **Relevance:** Teachers use Jamie's strengths and interests to support him to engage in class. His love of art and drama is used to support him in a range of other subjects. This motivates him and gives him confidence to tackle a wide range of subjects that he would otherwise feel were not relevant to him.

- **Response:** Jamie is given opportunities to engage throughout the lesson and share his learning with others using a range of resources, including IT software. He is given pre-warning of questions, so that he is able to plan and practise his response before he shares it with the class.

- **Recall:** Jamie uses a visual dictionary to support him to recall key words from each lesson. This is supported by visual prompts developed through pre- and over-learning.

- **Retention:** Jamie is supported to use visual prompts and, through pre- and over-learning, retain his understanding. Explicit links to his interests help to make this memorable for him.

- **Resilience:** Over the years, Jamie has learned to ask for specific help, and to engage in opportunities to work independently. He has learned that he will not be punished for getting it wrong; rather, he will be praised for trying.

The inclusive classroom checklist

We have developed a useful and simple checklist based on the eight Rs to help you develop an inclusive and effectively differentiated classroom. Mark your classroom out of ten for each of the following points and write down things you will change for any areas you identify as needing improvement. Ten is a model of excellence and one means you need to take action as soon as possible. You can download a printable copy of this checklist at www.bloomsbury.com/the-inclusive-classroom.

		/10	Actions I will take
ROOM The learning space needs to reflect needs and promote engagement. Classrooms need to hold space for physical, sensory, cognitive and emotional needs of all inhabitants – children and adults alike.	Can all children see whatever they need to see (board, teacher, learning materials, etc.)?		
	Can they all hear?		
	Is the light too bright?		
	Does the seating plan take into account different children's needs?		
	Is the room physically accessible to all children (and adults)?		
RELATIONSHIPS Relationships are key to successful inclusive teaching. The adults in the room need to know their children and the different ways of relating to them.	Does every vulnerable child have a go-to trusted adult they can turn to? Do they know who that is?		
	Do you know who has attachment and SEMH issues in your classroom?		
	Do you know how to respond to the attachment and SEMH needs of the children in your classroom?		
	Do you know which children can support or distract each other?		
RESOURCES It's easy to 'buy' a lot of materials and we don't suggest this. Resources imply minimal, simple and effective materials that support personalised access to learning rather than make up for it. Poor resources could be ready-made worksheets. A good resource might be a cushion for a child with dyspraxia.	Are there resources needed for children to support their access to reading and writing?		
	Can you utilise resources to support other needs, such as sensory, physical and emotional needs?		
	Are visual prompts readily available and used effectively?		

	/10	Actions I will take
RESOURCES (CONTINUED)	Have you discussed the resources with the children? Are they interested in actually using the ones you suggest? Are they confident to choose their own?		
	Are children encouraged to use resources to further their independence? Are they able to organise themselves?		
RELEVANCE How well do you adapt the curriculum to your children? Does your teaching inspire and draw in your children because they feel it relates to them or is useful? Does the curriculum engage their enthusiasm and participation?	How far does the learning and curriculum relate to children's own experiences?		
	Are children supported to make links between their experiences outside the classroom and their learning?		
	How far is the curriculum adapted to reflect local needs and issues?		
	Does the curriculum include an awareness of anxiety triggers for individual children (e.g. talk of family trees for looked-after children)?		
RESPONSE Are our instructions and guidance differentiated to different children? Are the questions and answers between adult and child adapted to meet the needs of the children? Does the adult demonstrate understanding of the child through their language?	Are *all* children supported to contribute to their own and the class's learning?		
	Do adult responses support children to engage with learning and develop perseverance and resilience?		
	Are children allowed time to process and develop their thinking before they are expected to share learning?		
	Are children encouraged to share their learning in different ways, including the use of technology?		
	Do the adults understand how to adapt their responses to children and do this effectively?		

	/10	Actions I will take
RECALL You may have taught an amazing lesson but what have the children retained? How do you know? Do you support children with working memory issues?	Do you use questioning and a variety of prompts to support children in recalling and applying their learning?		
	Are children able to share the recall of their learning in different ways (e.g. not always expecting them to write it down)?		
	Are you able to support the children to understand which bits of the learning and exercises are relevant to remember?		
RETENTION Do you know what your children recall a couple of weeks after the lesson? What are the students retaining to be able to apply later?	Are there regular opportunities for children to revisit learning to support their long-term understanding?		
	How far are children supported to see how different pieces of learning relate to each other and fit together?		
	Are children enabled to practise and develop a range of skills across the curriculum?		
RESILIENCE Are the children supported to feel OK to try and fail and then feel confident enough to try again? Does the support you provide for children in your classroom build further independence or does it simply sort out a temporary problem by creating a dependence on an adult such as a TA or LSA?	How far are children, especially those with SEN, supported and given opportunities for independent working?		
	Are they prompted for independence rather than encouraged to become dependent on adult prompts?		
	Is there a culture within the classroom where it is acceptable to make mistakes, and are these seen as learning opportunities?		
	How far does teacher feedback enable children to identify and celebrate success, rather than just identify areas for development?		

Conclusion

There's a jarring message for some in our conclusions: not every SEN child needs the entire lesson to be specialised. This is a radical departure from the norm and the expectation. There are two reasons, as we have stated above:

1. They may just need a very quick and simple adjustment here, while another child needs a different bit of the lesson adapted and so on.
2. Teachers simply do not have the time to differentiate everything throughout the whole lesson.

In the end, it boils down to good routines and practices that do not take up much time but are rich in maximising children's engagement and that sense of 'I belong and can be successful in this class'. We hope our book will support you in achieving this.

How to use this book

Case study: Callum

Callum was a sweet boy to speak to one-on-one, but he didn't like lessons, except for music. He was consistent and predictable in the way he distracted his peers and annoyed his teachers. He was told off by everybody throughout the day. There was a second application for an EHCP in the pipeline and the education psychologist had written some advice for his teachers. None of the staff were able to implement the very long list of advice, or they had tried elements of it for months without success.

This book offers workable tweaks and adaptations for teachers to use to create an inclusive environment with the least effort, time and stress possible. We do this by breaking down the lesson into manageable 'phases' to enable teachers to set up a series of routines and good practice that will help them to differentiate throughout their teaching for the benefit of all children.

Take, for example, the first phase: entering the classroom. We tend to think of this as a small point, but for the more challenging and vulnerable children this is where it can all go right or wrong. We are not looking for an extensive 'entering the class' differentiation but some simple and quick routines. For example, let's give Callum a 'hello' as he comes through the door and some praise for a 'role' he has been given, helping the other children settle and making sure everyone has the right equipment. The purpose of this time and stress-free intervention is to begin every lesson positively for Callum. That can impact on the way he feels about the lesson he is about to experience. 'Getting it right' in inclusion usually has one simple metric: enabling the children to engage with the lesson (preferably confidently and calmly). With this in mind, we need to think about setting the children up for a series of small successes throughout the lesson.

The five phases of the lesson

We have broken the lesson down into five phases and each chapter focuses on one specific phase and its priorities. We regard the phases as a series of routines that work for most, if not all, children, and each one requires only a minimum time input. You could read these phases as a roadmap to small successes throughout the class experience, particularly for the most vulnerable and challenging children. Here are the five phases:

PHASE 1: Transition, entering the classroom and preparing to learn

a. What happens before the children enter, including the attitude of the teacher: 'supporting' rather than penalising children and starting on a positive note.
b. Seating plans and starting routines: being simple and clear, removing uncertainty, and use of visual timetables.

PHASE 2: Delivering and receiving instructions and whole-class engagement

a. Making sure the message you communicate is understood by giving effective instructions that reduce barriers of misunderstanding, for example providing visual or written as well as verbal instructions.
b. Using prompt questions effectively to avoid confusion, for example avoiding vague, unclear statements that are open to interpretation and confusion.

PHASE 3: Individuals working as a class

a. Making writing and production of 'work' more accessible and avoiding the dreaded 'boredom by worksheet'.
b. Managing the distractions and interruptions, including working silently versus self-talk.

PHASE 4: Individuals fitting into a group of learners

a. Balancing groups of students, considering the demands of social and academic skills and guided by the use of explicit roles and rules for working together.
b. Managing sensory and concentration level issues and their impact, for example is this group too loud or not loud enough for the child?

PHASE 5: The last five minutes

a. Enabling the child to identify learning through self- and peer-assessment and to clarify understanding through over-learning.
b. Providing a clear end to the lesson with pre-warning and clear routines and leaving the room calmly with praise and positivity.

How this works in practice

Now let's return to Callum. If we start by getting him into the classroom calmly, we are setting the stage for a better start to the lesson. Key to this is getting Callum calmly from the playground to the classroom (phase 1). He is met at the entrance from the playground and helped to come through the building to the classroom, reducing the sensory overload of the corridors and allowing him to be talked through what will happen in the lesson to come. He has a clear routine while the class settles. He hands out books and other equipment, which makes him feel valued and allows him to scan the room for 'dangers'. The whole-class visual timetable reminds him what to expect during the lesson.

Callum uses a whiteboard to record his ideas, so he doesn't forget them during the whole-class engagement, which reduces his shouting out. This also stops him fiddling. He knows that he will be called upon at some point in the lesson and the teacher tries to give him a pre-warning of when that might be (phase 2).

As he is calmer, more focused and feels more secure and valued in the room, Callum is able to tackle individual or group tasks with a minimal check from an adult, who supports his understanding of the task and provides him with a task-management board. In Callum's case this is a list of the tasks to be completed (used by numerous others in the class as well), with a little sketch by it to make it easier for him to identify the task without having to read the list fully. This helps him stay on task. He enjoys ticking off the different tasks as he completes them. This reassures him that he is making progress and is doing the right thing. It also means that he doesn't need constantly to get adult reassurance by shouting out, which enables him and others to focus better. Also, when he loses focus, he is able to use the list to refocus himself without disrupting others (phases 3 and 4).

At the end of the lesson, an adult checks in with Callum to help him identify something positive from the lesson to enable him to start the next lesson feeling confident and secure (phase 5).

By embedding differentiation into each phase of the lesson, we can support Callum to engage with the learning and save ourselves work in managing disruptions to the lesson. There's no big time-consuming adaptation here, as you might have expected. The rest of the book explains how to add to and develop this.

Final point

We've said it already so this is just a reiteration: the biggest barriers for effective inclusion are time, stress and money. It would be much to our chagrin if you read this book feeling overwhelmed by how much more you now have to do. We would have failed categorically in our endeavour. So, please use this book to find simpler and easier ways of doing the wonderful work you already do. By no means do we ever suggest that you 'have to' do something or you are 'judged badly if you don't'. We have included our top tips, so choose a handful, try them out, and see whether they work for you and your children. See how you can adapt them to fit your circumstances. You have permission to try new things along the same lines. Don't try to do *everything* in this book – do what is going to work for you and make your life easier, not harder.

1 Phase 1 of the lesson: Transition, entering the classroom and preparedness to learn

After his poem 'Cause I Ain't Got a Pencil' went viral on social media, American poet Joshua T. Dickerson gave an interview to explain that he wrote it after learning about a scenario where a child asked his teacher for a pencil. The teacher said he could have a pencil if he gave one of his shoes as a deposit. The child removed his shoe to reveal a dirty sock, causing the other children in the class to laugh. 'I wrote a story about what I imagined happened prior to that moment,' Dickerson said. If you don't know the poem, it's worth searching online for it.

The point for us is that no child enters the classroom as a blank page. What has happened before they entered your classroom will influence how they respond to what happens there. We can't fix all the ills of society that our children have to endure, however deeply we feel that we want to. But we can make children's experience of our classrooms successful for both them and us. This starts with how children enter our classrooms or 'the transition'. We can make a huge difference to how the whole lesson will go and, arguably, how this child's and your day will go with a smooth and calm transition that is awake to all the possibilities of what happened prior to them entering your domain.

Three types of lesson entrance

The first type of lesson entrance describes most of my teachers: they made us line up in silence before entering the room in absolute silence and getting the gravest of punishments if you dared to mess around during the start of the lesson. Books had to be on the table, and we all had to be ready to learn. Only when the teacher said the simple word 'Sit' did we do this quickly, and immediately the lesson began.

There was one maths teacher who never followed through on his threats, so when we barged in laughing and shoving to his unheard and unheeded shouts of 'Quietly please', his lesson continued to be a behavioural nightmare.

There was another teacher who let us wander in and settle at our own pace but at a certain point it was clear that he expected silence and dealt with us like a comedian putting down a heckler if we didn't comply. He made up mocking but hilarious poems about us on the spot and his authority was from both a superior intellect but also a kindness through humour. We had respect for this man partly because he was a bit of an enigma but also because he actually enabled us to enjoy the class through his quirky humour, which was anathema in that school.

Daniel

These memories represent your three archetypal starts to the traditional lesson, each with their flaws and benefits. They are all predicated on the teacher – not the child. Throughout the course of the lesson, the entrance to the classroom took its toll. The mood set at the beginning was a marker for how this lesson would go and what you could expect from the teachers. The super authoritarian easily lost children, who would simply lie or pretend to be keeping up with the lesson so as not to fall victim to his punishment. The zero structure and follow-through maths teacher enabled the children to experience a lot of merriment, mockery and bullying but very little maths. The cool teacher had his off-days, but the joy of the class was largely followed up with an enthusiasm for learning. Either way, how the children entered the class would determine the mood of the rest of the lesson and this remains true in almost every setting in the world. 'Start as you mean to go on' is not a life lesson we can claim to have invented. However, we can tell you that all children, but especially the most vulnerable, distressed, challenging and awkward children, benefit significantly from us getting the entrance right. Furthermore, the majority of cases where significant interruptions happen are rooted in negative behaviours and inattentive engagement traceable back to how the lesson started for that child. But don't worry, it's not rocket science. It is very doable.

Consider the archetypal but fictitious case of Ryan and Ms Murphy. Ryan bursts into the classroom with a zealous hyperactivity inversely proportionate to his ability to participate in the lesson. As his teacher, Ms Murphy's cortisol levels spike and she thinks of the after-school drink she's promised herself. 'No, this is your seat,' she shouts at him as he tussles with Ali over the chair near the window. As soon as he sits down, Ryan gets up again, grabs Monique's pen and holds it up in the air protesting, 'Miss, Miss, this is MY pen.' Ms Murphy screams, 'Sit down and shut up!' She remembers how much she hates Ryan. Ryan sits momentarily until the lesson begins, when he gets up again – 'I'm trying to find my pen, Miss,' he says, which is met with the exhaustedly frustrated reply: 'RYAN! GET OUT!'

Most people reading this are thinking about Ryan but we also need to think about Ms Murphy's mental health and wellbeing. A bugbear of ours (and a major motivation for writing this book) is that our teaching profession is producing too many Ms Murphys and Ryans and not asking enough compassionate questions about either.

We have heard the view too many times that Ms Murphy needs to work harder, be better or even that she should leave the profession because she is simply not good enough. Equally, we know there is a whole movement of teachers who would suggest that the Ryans of this world need to be removed from the mainstream classroom, so teachers can focus on the children who really want to be there and learn. We are exhausted by the astounding levels of ignorance and vehemence in this argument. We don't have time to thrash this policy approach out in any depth in this book but, simply, we will proceed on the assumption that you want to try to include all students wherever possible as long as they are not a danger to themselves or others. So, let's briefly consider perhaps the most important element to this point: we are dealing with two human beings who both have needs. It's possible that seeing this same scenario from different perspectives may be driven by the level of emotional intelligence one has. Either way, here are the questions that are worth asking about both of these people:

- How is Ms Murphy doing? What do we know about her life and whatever else is going on for her? Who is there to help her out with her own personal circumstances? Is there any emotional support her more senior colleagues can offer her?

- How can senior colleagues help Ms Murphy by destressing her workload, upskilling, supporting, befriending, caring and so on?

- What else is going on for Ryan at home or at school that we need to know about? How is he doing? How does he feel about school? How does he feel about himself?

These very simple, basic questions are not motivated by any fancy policy or 'wellbeing approach' or any other fad, but simply one human concern for another. There is a theme in all SEN or pastoral work that our Inclusion Expert team apply and that is: have you gone over and spoken to the child (and if you're a senior member of staff observing the lesson, the teacher)? Before we get to any of the top tips below, step number one – and not because this is part of your job description but simply because you are a caring person – has to be to go and speak with them non-judgementally. We hope this point is redundant; however, based on our team's experience and involvement with thousands of children and teachers across the UK and abroad, we know this often doesn't happen. Unfortunately, the national data around teachers leaving the profession and citing stress doesn't bring much hope (Department for Education, 2020). At the heart of this scenario is an expression of care and emotional intelligence; the rest of this book is the detail.

Returning to the story of Ryan and Ms Murphy, there are two priorities, regardless of the detail of Ryan's SEN profile, that need to be addressed: his preparedness for learning and his ability to 'settle'. Unless Ryan can participate in the first ten minutes of the class (at least), we cannot support his other needs and learning. We would argue that Ryan's diagnosis is not relevant; the concern is to identify and meet his needs and enable him to settle to learn effectively. Ms Murphy needs to both understand and remember that, however irritating and frustrating Ryan's behaviour is, it is unlikely to be deliberately designed to wind her up. Behaviour is communication; when we don't have or can't use words for our feelings, we communicate through our behaviour.

So, what is Ryan communicating? It could be anxiety, frustration or even excitement about what has happened before he came into the room, be that playing football at break, a successful science lesson, a period of exclusion in the deputy head's office, an argument at home or simply navigating a crowded corridor to reach the classroom. All these events and many more will influence Ryan's behaviour before he even reaches the classroom door.

Once he enters the room, he has to manage a whole new set of questions and emotions arising in response to them. Where do I sit? What is going to happen in this lesson? Will I be able to understand what I need to do? Will I fail? Will I look stupid? Will others laugh at me? Do I want others to laugh at me? If they are laughing at me, does that mean they are my friends? Will I get any help with my learning? Just managing this internal dialogue is exhausting and stressful, particularly when the thought that 'Ms Murphy hates me' is added. Ryan will know that she is stressed by him, even if he can't understand or name her emotion. Her anxiety about his presence will add to Ryan's anxiety, setting off a vicious circle of negative emotion.

Ms Murphy needs to try to see those first few moments from Ryan's point of view and then support him to manage that maelstrom of emotion. By changing the narrative of that transition, she can begin to reclaim her classroom and control of the lesson. In general, we can assume that all children thrive on routine, predictability and, most importantly, clarity. Even though she may feel that 'I told them and they should remember what is happening', even in the most able groups there are those who will struggle with this, adding to their anxiety and negatively impacting their behaviour and learning.

The message is that clear and explicit routines support transition into the classroom by removing uncertainty and therefore stress for children and teachers.

Top tips for effective settling

With this in mind, here are our top tips for building routines into the first few minutes of a lesson to help settle a class effectively.

Tip 1: Meet and greet

There are a vast range of internet videos of classes of primary school children being greeted by manically grinning teachers with hugs, fist bumps and high fives. This is not necessarily what we mean by meet and greet. We mean for the teacher to stand by the door and greet the children with a smile and a warm, friendly 'Hello. How are you?' to make them feel welcome and wanted. Also, this gives the teacher an opportunity to assess the child's emotional state and readiness to learn and plan their response.

Instead of this...	... try this
You ask all your children to stand in silence by the door, then when – and only when – they are all silent, order them to enter the room, without making eye contact with any of them.	As the children arrive, smile and welcome them into the room, making eye contact with all those willing to give it to you. This brief contact can set the tone for the lesson and allows them and you to see each other as human.

Case study: Mr Green and Mrs Brown

Mr Green teaches in a small primary school where they have a 'soft' start. The children need to be in school by 9.00 am but can enter the classroom any time between 8.45 am and 9.00 am. Mr Green resents this. He is annoyed that the soft start eats into his planning (and coffee) time. So, throughout this time, he sits at his desk and ignores the children, except to bark at them periodically to put their coats away and read in silence. Equally, they ignore him and his demands. By 9.00 am, Mr Green is cross and frustrated, and the children are overexcited and noisy. Oddly, his first lesson does not go well.

By contrast, Mrs Brown stands by the door from 8.45 am for five or so minutes, greeting the children and chatting to any parents who come to the door. The children know the routine to get on with reading quietly. As Mrs Brown moves from the door, she goes over and checks in with her most vulnerable pupils. The children know that she will move around the room, so that they will be able to share any important information about the previous evening with her as a trusted adult. By 9.00 am, all is calm and the children are ready for the day.

Tip 2: Plan a clear and consistent starting routine for the lesson

This could be a simple activity that can help Ryan or any other child settle – it could be that Ms Murphy hands him a word search, which he loves doing, the moment he walks in the room (she might need to give him a pen as well). A 'settling task' that a child likes is a way of cutting through the whole process of having to get ready, unpack, sit in their seat and settle, which many find a struggle. Ideally this is the same routine every lesson, unless the teacher has pre-warned them in advance, or if that fails at the door, of a change. This takes time to establish but is worth it.

Instead of this...	... try this
The whole class enters the room and is expected to get out their books and other equipment, then sits looking at the teacher ready to work. However, it takes ten minutes to achieve this.	As the class enters the room, they collect one of three familiar starting tasks from the table by the door, or start on the task displayed on the board. The teacher gives particular children individual tasks that will meet their particular needs, such as a calming activity or a reminder of the vocabulary from the previous lesson. Everyone knows what to do and the lesson starts quickly and calmly.

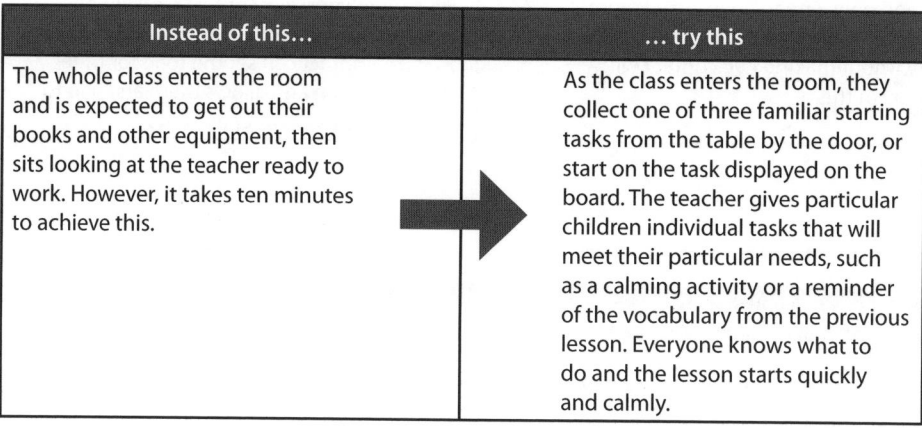

It can help to display a slide on the board – it can be the same basic one every lesson – to act as a reminder as the children come in of the clear, simple and accessible settling tasks. Using visual prompts to remind children of the regular tasks is a great time-saver.

Tip 3: Don't set up impossible expectations

Too often we set up expectations for the start of lessons that are difficult and stressful to meet. This can be things like coming into class silently. This means that any child who makes a noise, even an apology for bumping into someone else, has immediately fallen foul of the expectation. Further, any child who wishes to wind their teacher up just needs to make a slight but significant, and ideally hard-to-identify, noise to achieve this. Equally, the teacher is expected to deal with all these different infringements, which adds to their stress and distracts from the focus of learning. As we have discussed, a calm routine for entering the room is key, but the expectations must be manageable and reasonable.

This issue is often exacerbated by schools that set routines for their staff for the start of the day or the lesson that can only lead to stress and non-compliance. For example, the expectation that the class will enter the classroom at 8.55 am: the teacher will need to do the register, check dinners, hear three daily readers, deal with lost property and an irate parent, and then start a maths lesson at 9.05 am. This can't be done. The result is a stressed and ineffective response to all the tasks.

If we want teaching to be effective, we need to start calmly.

Instead of this...	... try this
As the class comes in, you try to catch up with three children about their incomplete homework, speak to another about the previous lesson as they missed it, and organise the rest of the class to start reading Chapter 6 while ensuring that all the laptops are turned on. All this needs to be completed in three minutes or the lesson will start late.	Have a pre-loaded slide on the board into which you can insert the information for the start of the lesson. This could include: • giving the instructions for the starting activity ('Read Chapter 6') • identifying the child or group of children you need to speak to • asking a named child to set up the laptops. This takes a moment or two to set up, but once the children are used to the routine, it provides a calmer start to the lesson. Also, it makes the expectations more manageable.

Tip 4: A role in the room

An easy way of achieving both a sense of predictable routine and making a child feel that they are important to this class is to give the child a job to do at the beginning of the class. It could be to hand out any materials or work on the teacher's desk or to set up the laptops as in the example above. This makes the child feel good, supports them to settle and could provide some 'heavy load' work to help meet their sensory needs.

Instead of this...	... try this
You walk around the room giving out the books, explaining the task as you go. You are aware that you're losing your place in the explanation as you look at the badly written names and try to avoid falling over a bag and remember what you are saying simultaneously. Equally, the children are struggling to follow what you are saying as they swivel their heads to follow you around the room like spectators at a tennis match or just give up.	You know that Jed needs a regular movement break, so you get him to give out the books each lesson while you stand at the front explaining what to do next, supported by the visual on the board. As you are doing this, you notice that Oli and Martha are both a bit fidgety today, so you give them another quick job involving movement before they start their learning task.

Tip 5: Consider a staggered start

We all know that trying to get anywhere through a crowd is stressful. Consider then what navigating their way into the classroom feels like for a child with sensory issues, or for a child whose social interaction difficulties mean that they struggle to differentiate between being punched and bumped in the general melee of the corridor. For these children, simply getting into the room is so stressful that learning becomes a virtual impossibility. For these children, coming into a room separately can make a huge difference.

Case study: Jakub

Jakub struggled to manage change and his sensory issues made a school corridor full of people very hard for him to manage. If asked to come in with everyone else, Jakub would have a meltdown as he entered the school building. Then he would be so distressed that he spent most of the rest of the day in the SENCO's office sobbing intermittently and learning nothing. Quickly, it was agreed that Jakub should come into school five minutes early and go straight to his classroom while it was still quiet. However, the transition from his foster carer to the teacher was still too much, so an additional supportive element had to be provided. Jakub loved to use the paper cutter (under supervision for health and safety reasons!). So, it was agreed that each morning Jakub would come in early and trim all the resources for the day. This gave him a sense of value and self-worth and provided the sensory calming activity that enabled him to make a successful transition to the quiet classroom. Once his classmates were in the room and settled, Jakub was able to leave the paper cutter and take his seat at the back of the room.

Jakub's example is an extreme case. Often a quick assessment at the door will be enough for the teacher to identify that a particular child needs five minutes' calm time before they start the lesson. There are various ways to provide this, including:

- letting the child into the room first so that they can find their seat and sort themselves out when it is quiet
- a walk up and down the now-calm corridor
- sitting at the back of the class with a book or drawing a picture
- standing outside the room until they feel ready to come in
- taking a 'message' to another member of staff.

The use of such strategies needs to be agreed as school policy, so that the child is neither found by a member of the senior leadership team (SLT) in the 'wrong place' and told off, nor fearful that this will happen.

Instead of this...	... try this
Harry arrives at the classroom door almost literally 'bouncing off the walls', and you hustle him into the room, shouting for him to sit down. His classmates stare and snigger, which increases his anxiety and your stress. Things move rapidly from bad to worse and five minutes into the lesson, you call for SLT to remove Harry from the lesson as now he is throwing things.	You can see Harry is over-excited, anxious and in no state to learn. You identify these feelings for him quietly, calmly and away from other children. You reassure Harry that you do want him in the lesson, but he needs to get himself ready to learn first. You agree that he will take a pile of books to a teacher in another room. This provides Harry with both some quiet time and some 'heavy load' work to help him calm. When Harry returns, you ask him whether he feels ready to start learning yet. It may be that he will need more time out before he is able to settle.

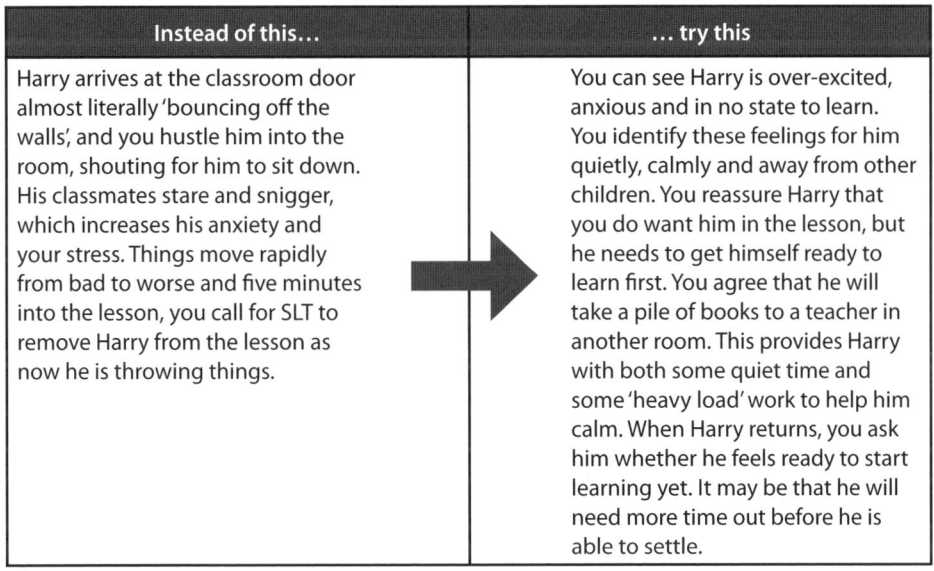

Considering the room

Classrooms are tricky places. As with any communal space, they need to fulfil a wide range of different functions and meet the different needs of different people at the same time. This creates a range of challenges.

This is increased in secondary schools, where the same space will be used by a variety of different year groups with different learning needs and curricula. Sometimes the classroom 'belongs' to a particular teacher and sometimes the room will be used by a variety of staff, often, but not always, within the same faculty. In these cases, there are particular issues about adapting the room to the needs of a particular group of pupils or an individual pupil.

In primary schools, usually the teacher and the class are in the room for the majority of their lessons. This can make the implementation of adaptations for groups or individuals easier. However, the length of time that they are in the room can create its own difficulties and challenges.

Whatever the situation, when considering the environment of the classroom and its impact on the children and their learning, there is much that is beyond the teacher's control – the size and shape of the room, the number of display boards, the arrangement of the windows, the temperature and light. But what is key is to be aware of these issues and consider their impact on the children in the room and their learning.

Physical, sensory, visual and auditory

In all cases, making the classroom work as a learning space will be a compromise between different children's (and the teacher's) needs and the physical limitations of the room.

> *I remember many years ago being told that I had to have a working wall for each of reading, writing and maths, which must be interactive, at the children's eye height and at the front of the room, plus a celebration board, a book corner with supporting display, an information board and various other things. The only problem was it couldn't be done. There were only four boards in the whole room; none were at the front or at the children's eye height.*
>
> *Sara*

These are real-life limitations we need to work with to provide the best working environment for our children. It is about adaptations and a flexible approach, not commandments set in stone. When we look at the classroom, we need to balance the often conflicting demands of the curriculum, school policy, the needs of the children and the physical limits of the room. If we fail to create a space that is supportive of the children's learning, we are on a hiding to nothing.

Throughout this book, we emphasise the importance of visual supports and prompts to facilitate children to access learning and classroom routines. But we are aware that too many of these messages can quickly become overwhelming. We need to work to ensure that our displays are accessible, relevant and useful. There are many books written about class displays full of creative ideas, but from our point of view the key question is: 'Does the display support learning?' Furthermore, we need to ensure that it is not hindering learning.

Case study: Ms Patel

Ms Patel was an amazingly creative teacher with a background in art and years of experience of creating window designs for department stores. Each half term, she would spend several days revamping her class to match the coming half term's topics. An Amazon rainforest would sprout over her walls or the room could resemble a Palaeolithic cave complete with cave paintings and dinosaur bones. They were truly works of art. Certainly, the children were excited to see what each new term would bring, but the impact was short lived. Many struggled to focus and concentrate among the swaying and brightly coloured objects. Others found that the poor light in the room impacted their focus. The children found it hard to find the information they needed – key vocabulary and modelled examples – hidden among the many visual images. It was not clear whom these displays were for or who benefited from them. Ms Patel was stressed by trying to realise her ever more grandiose plans and they inhibited rather than supported the children's learning.

Instead of this...	... try this
To support the children's learning and provide as many visual prompts as possible, you cover every wall and even parts of the windows with key vocabulary, reminders of formulae and grammatical structures, mostly downloaded from one of the many websites devoted to producing such resources. The result is visually overwhelming, and it is virtually impossible to find anything in the vast array of information. The displays become a 'wallpaper' of inaccessible information.	Select a few pieces of key information relevant for each subject, colour-coded so that they are easy to spot, to make up the permanent supporting display. Then use flip chart sheets to display the information needed for this lesson. Previous sheets can be kept for the duration of the topic pegged to a hanger as a 'reference source' to act as a reminder of the previous work and a support for over-learning.

For many children, when it comes to display, less is more. If we wish them to focus on learning, we need to avoid filling the classroom with unnecessary distractions that make it harder for them to concentrate. We need to focus on making the environment as supportive as possible, balancing the competing demands of stimulation, support for focus and prompts for learning. There is no magic formula for this, and the balance will vary from class to class and room to room.

Sitting comfortably

Going back to the 1960s and 1970s, *Listen with Mother*, the groundbreaking storytelling programme on BBC Radio, started each episode with the line: 'Is everyone sitting comfortably? Then we shall begin.' This is more than a comforting refrain; it is a key piece of advice for getting and keeping an audience's attention. If we want children to listen, we need to ensure that they are comfortable. We all know how difficult it is to focus when we are not comfortable.

Too often in classrooms we ask children to sit on chairs that are too big or too small or to sit on the floor when it is not comfortable. Few of us are able to sit cross-legged for any length of time without a back support, yet we ask primary school children to do this for significant periods of time.

Case study: Clara

Clara has hypermobility. Sitting still for any length of time is hard. Sitting without support is even harder. Yet she is eager to please and not appear different, so when her class sits on the floor, she does so too. However, the sheer effort of remaining upright takes all her focus and attention. This means that she cannot listen to the teacher at the same time. It took a long time for her teacher to realise that the reason why Clara was taking in so little of what was being taught during the input was because all her focus was being put into staying upright. She made a quick change so that a group of children always sat on chairs. This group included Clara, even when others were swapped around, which meant her back was supported, she felt included and she was able to focus on her learning.

Instead of this...	... try this
All the tables and chairs in the classroom match, regardless of the size of the children.	Swap with other teachers so that you have a variety of furniture in your room and the children can sit at a table and chair that are the right size for them. Where this is not possible, a cushion to raise a child up to the table height or a box or upturned tray to rest their feet on will support them to sit comfortably and focus better.

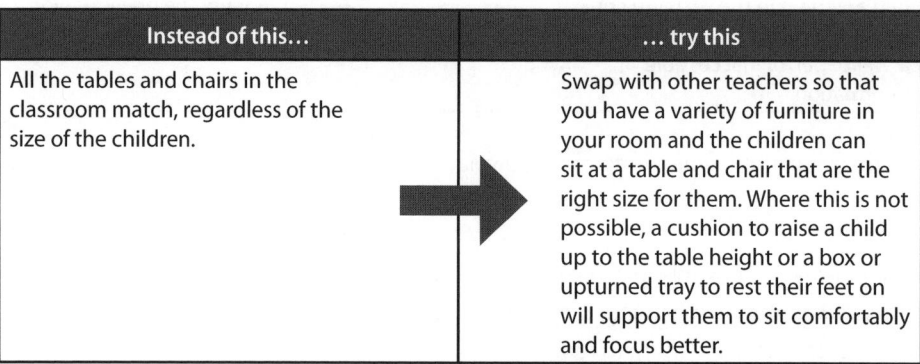

Don't underestimate the importance of sitting comfortably. The following tips will help you to ensure that children are able to concentrate in your lessons.

Tip 1: Children need to be taught explicitly the rules about sitting on the carpet, or indeed on a chair

At home, for very young children, sitting and listening or watching the television is a time to cuddle up to others, lean or lie down. This is right and appropriate at home, but not in school. These expectations need to be made clear. Not all children pick this up automatically. So often we say that we expect 'good sitting' but are not explicit about what this means. This needs to be modelled, a visual prompt provided to remind the children of the expectation and those who model it should be praised explicitly, for example: 'Well done for sitting with your legs crossed.' For some children, the visual prompt will need to be personalised; try a photograph of them modelling the expectation, which can be shown to them to remind them both of the expectation and that they can achieve it.

Tip 2: Managing personal space

One of the implicit expectations of children about sitting in any crowded space is an understanding of how much space they need to leave between them and the next person – side to side, behind and in front – so they don't sit on or squash others. For children with poor coordination or social understanding, this needs to be supported, explained and modelled.

For children with sensory issues, the amount of personal space they need may be different to others. This can be supported by:

- Use of PE hoops. By placing a hoop over the child, you can build a visual image of their and others' personal space and set up the rule that you need to ask to enter another's personal space in school.
- Tape to mark each child's working space on shared tables. For some, a piece of A4 card attached to the table at the appropriate angle and distance from them acts as a useful reminder of where to place their book, to support them to work without infringing on others' space.

Remember, for a child with coordination difficulties, remaining within a set space can be physically difficult.

Tip 3: Allow children to find a comfortable way to sit

We tend to tell children to cross their legs when they sit on the floor. But this is not comfortable for all children and is not always appropriate for those wearing skirts. We need to consider the best way for the individual to sit, balancing their comfort and others' needs to be able to see and also sit comfortably. As discussed above, if all your effort is focused on maintaining a sitting position, you can't focus on learning. It is worth considering more imaginative responses. Do all the children need to sit at all? Could some be standing at the back, lying down or allowed to walk the room before settling?

Seating plans

For many children, one of the numerous uncertainties on entering the classroom is where to sit. There is a highly complex social etiquette about who sits with whom and when.

A seating plan reduces uncertainty and thus stress for children, while providing an element of control for the teacher. If we return to the story of Ryan from page 35, his difficulty with finding the correct seat and the ensuing conflict with Ms Murphy raised the stress levels of them both before the lesson had even started. Ms Murphy can reduce Ryan's stress by having a seating plan and sticking to it. Ryan may need to be reminded where he sits as he comes in. This needs to be a clear, polite instruction, not a request, as that provides ambiguity and room for confusion.

We appreciate that the average classroom seating plan is very complicated and best done using a computer borrowed from NASA. A successful seating plan will position the children so that they are best placed to understand and access our communication and teaching. We need to start by considering whether the child can see and hear from where they are sitting. This is more than checking those who have hearing and sight impairments are sitting in the most appropriate place, though this is very important. It is also considering other issues, like height. All too often in attempts to avoid sitting the gossipers and the disruptors together, we miss that we have sat Josh, who is one metre tall, behind Robert, who is two metres tall and nearly as wide. Result: Josh can't see and is quickly likely to disengage from learning.

Next consider the other issues that would impact your focus and concentration. Remember, these issues will apply to the children in your class. Have you sat the child who never wears a coat, even when it is snowing, next to the radiator? Or the child who wears a hat, coat and scarf, regardless of the season, by the window you have to keep open to clear the smell of the toilets? Consider not only the temperature of your room as a whole but the microclimates within it. There are children within most classes who will really appreciate both the 'hot' and 'cold' spots and whose engagement will be supported by sitting in them.

Further, consider who you position by the door or window. Those with poor focus may work better away from the distraction of the window. For the most easily distracted, you want to minimise the distraction between them and the point where you wish them to focus – you and the board. However, for the child with bladder issues who needs extra toilet breaks, if you sit them near the door so they can slip out without drawing attention to themselves, they are more likely to be able to relax and engage in learning. This equally applies for those who need to take regular movement breaks.

Finally, consider whether the child can see what they need to see without twisting, stretching and straining themselves and reach the materials they need at the same time. If not, are they able to move? And do they understand that they can move to see better? For many children, if they are told to stay in their seat and not move, they will assume that this applies at all times, regardless of whether they are moving so that they are more able to learn. Before you tell a child off for moving, it is always worth checking why they are moving and what message you are sending to the others about the need to move to learn.

Case study: Craig

Craig had a long experience of significant domestic abuse. He was living with his grandma as this was considered safer for him than living with either parent. He continued to have contact with both parents, even though his mum made it clear she would prefer to see his sister without him. Craig's behaviour in the classroom varied from violent and aggressive to quietly non-compliant. He had a particular resistance to any form of writing. The school SENCO was charged with getting him (and a large group of other vulnerable and under-achieving children) to achieve age expectations in English. The SENCO tried threatening, cajoling and bribing without any impact and adding to his and the SENCO's stress levels. The breakthrough came when the SENCO read Louise Michelle Bombèr's fabulous book, *Inside I'm Hurting* (2007), which looks at the experiences of children with attachment issues in the classroom and the adaptations that might support their learning. Slowly, she began to understand how unsafe the world might feel for Craig. Even though the classroom felt safe to the SENCO, it was still a place of threat and possible attack for Craig, which caused his aggressive outbursts. It was essential to make him feel safer so he could learn. The SENCO moved him to sit at the back of the room, allowing him to rock his chair so that his head touched the wall behind him. Slowly, over the following weeks, as he became confident that no one could get behind him and hurt him, his anxieties reduced and he became able to engage in learning and eventually even to commit his ideas to paper. He achieved age expectations. Such a simple seating change made so much difference.

Given the complications of the seating plan, there are those who question whether they are worth the bother. We would say an emphatic yes! For many who lack confidence or struggle with social communication or understanding, the seating plan is key to reducing their anxieties entering the room. It reduces the stress of finding a place or trying to understand the social etiquette of who sits next to whom. It gives a sense of security and order. It is important for primary school teachers and others who use the 'carpet' for input that a seating plan applies there too.

Instead of this…	… try this
The traditional classroom organisation is in ability groups with the less able sat with a TA, if you are lucky enough to have one.	Instead of looking at the groups of children and placing them according to their ability, look at them as individuals and consider where they would be best placed to support their learning and social development.

To help you develop and implement effective seating plans, we have compiled three top tips below.

Tip 1: Don't forget friendships

Developing friendships is an immensely important part of school life. It is important both that children are given opportunities to sit with their friends and that we understand and respect that there are those they do not want to sit near. Children's learning is supported by working with friends, and friendships are not based on ability. Equally, if you place a child next to someone who has bullied or upset them, this will inhibit their learning.

Tip 2: Ask the children

It is worth asking the children who they want to sit by and why. Even very young children may be aware that sometimes sitting next to their best friends is not always the best choice to support their learning. Children are often remarkably perceptive about the role of others to support their learning and may know more about their learning than we do!

Tip 3: Changing the seating plan

Because of the complications of seating plans, once we have something that works, we tend to regard it as set in stone. It shouldn't be. We need to adapt our plans for different activities and for different purposes. If we are going to work effectively with children, we will need to change the groups. Children may need different amounts of adult support for different subjects and even within subjects. Danielle may be your star pupil in number work but may need to sit near an adult for extra support when it comes to shape work. Most children are happy to change places for a lesson providing they can return to their home seat at the end of the lesson. But don't forget when you change the seating plan permanently to let the children know in advance that you are going to do it. If this is part of their sense of security in your classroom, you shouldn't change it without warning.

Supporting focus

Multi-professional colleagues often recommend fiddle toys or objects for children who have issues with focus and concentration and most teachers inwardly groan. There are many people whose focus is helped by fiddling. Watch any group of adults at a meeting; at least half will be fiddling, doodling or similar. The problem is we don't know how many of them are listening and how many are distracting the person next to them. The same is true of children. It is a really difficult balance between supporting the focus of some and managing the impact of that support in terms of the distraction of others, including the teacher or speaker.

The bottom line is that fiddling and movement help focus for many people, particularly those with ADHD (see Rotz and Wright, 2020). In fact, Sara is pretty sure that Daniel is not listening if he is still or only doing one thing. For him to focus fully, he needs to be doing several things at once. But for the speaker or teacher this is disconcerting. We expect focus and often believe if the listener is looking at us, they are listening to us. However, we need to remember that just because they are looking at us, it doesn't mean they are listening or understanding. Sometimes we need to challenge what we think of as focus and paying attention.

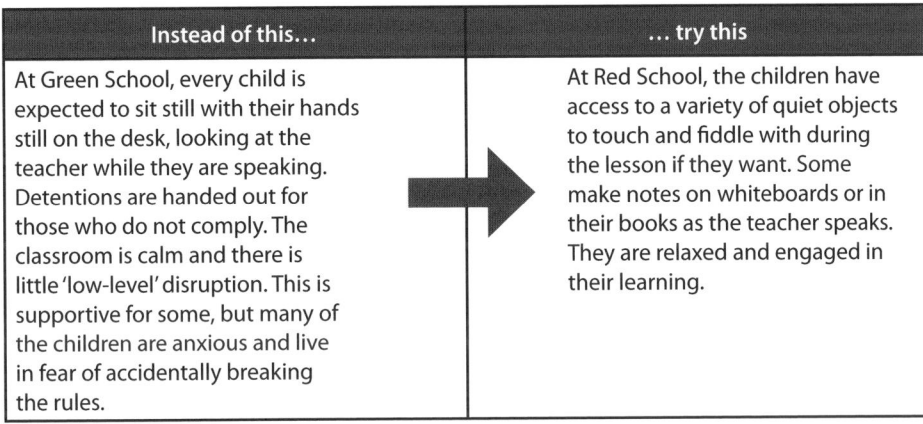

Instead of this...	... try this
At Green School, every child is expected to sit still with their hands still on the desk, looking at the teacher while they are speaking. Detentions are handed out for those who do not comply. The classroom is calm and there is little 'low-level' disruption. This is supportive for some, but many of the children are anxious and live in fear of accidentally breaking the rules.	At Red School, the children have access to a variety of quiet objects to touch and fiddle with during the lesson if they want. Some make notes on whiteboards or in their books as the teacher speaks. They are relaxed and engaged in their learning.

Top tips for working with those children who need to fiddle

So, how can we support children who do need to fiddle in order to concentrate and learn effectively? And how can we do that while minimising disruption for other children in the class? The following tips will offer some guidance.

1. Allow them to fiddle. It may be irritating for you, but it supports their learning. Consider who they sit near and their tolerance and level of distractibility.

2. If their fiddling distracts you from what you are teaching, sit the child to one side, out of your direct eyeline.

3. Try to make the fiddle objects small and quiet. Many of the commercially produced 'fiddle toys' are brightly coloured, shiny and even noisy. None of these are great for the classroom. Perhaps try to keep such things for when children are rewarded for completed work with fiddle time. In lessons, use quieter and smaller things, such as sticky tack (provided they are not going to eat it), loops of string, clothes pegs and cubes. For those with sensory issues, a strip of Velcro™ attached to the underside of the table for them to rub their fingers along can work well.

4. Consider what is on their desk. Anything that a child can reach will become something to fiddle with. Try to minimise the equipment that can be fiddled with. If it is a science lesson, don't set out anything breakable or dangerous in advance.

5. If the child is sitting on the carpet, they will use other children as fiddle objects. This can be minimised by sitting them at the front or at least not directly behind a child with long hair.

6. Use regular movement and fiddle breaks. The use of a gross motor movement break does not meet the same needs as the fine motor fiddling, but getting children to move regularly will help focus.

Supporting routines

Though the unexpected and surprises can be exciting, our sense of security is based on knowing what is going to happen next. It is only from a secure base that we are able to enjoy the unexpected. Knowing we are going to have dinner means that we can enjoy the anticipation of an unknown and possibly surprising sweet treat at the end of the meal; however, if we are uncertain whether we will receive any meal or what it will be like, this is a source of anxiety that can become overwhelming. Children who feel secure and understand and are able to predict what is going on around them are more able to deal with the unexpected. For many children, just entering the classroom with its wide range of unpredictable events, interactions and expectations is a huge source of anxiety, which impacts their learning, behaviour and wellbeing. These children need the day-to-day routines of the classroom to be made explicit and to be forewarned of the changes.

It is easy to feel that every day is basically the same, so why would children need this to be explained? We need to remember that we are the ones with the power to change it. Also, think how much we, as adults, are stressed by the unexpected – the fire alarm going off, the computers or photocopier not working or a visit from an inspector – or even a planned-for change like an outing, a visitor or a complex learning activity. In reality, few days or lessons in any school are 'always the same'; there is always change and the unexpected is a constant.

Case study: Thalia

Thalia loved to dress up and had a variety of favourite costumes, so she was excited at the prospect of wearing one of them to school for World Book Day. But as the day itself drew near, she became more and more anxious. Would people like her costume? Was it appropriate? Would people understand its link to a book? Would someone else be wearing the same costume? Would she be too hot or too cold in the costume? What other events would be happening that day? As these questions and many others whirled around in her head, Thalia became more and more anxious, began to scratch at her arms and chew her lips and eventually refused to go into school. The uncertainties of this much-anticipated event became too much.

Predictable, anxiety-free routines

We need to work to make the world of school more predictable for children who struggle to manage change or understand and process what is going on around them. The classic response to this is a visual timetable and these can be found at some level in most primary school classrooms, and the vast majority of secondary school pupils are provided with a timetable as standard.

Visual timetables

A visual timetable needs to be clear and visual. It does not need to be pictorial. As children become more confident readers, the pictures and symbols can be supplemented and then replaced with words. However, it's important to remember that just because a child is in secondary school, it does not mean that they can read (or process) a written timetable.

One of the advantages of using visual timetables is that they force us as adults to consider and plan for the day in a way that focuses us on how our pupils may perceive it. However, there are also a number of issues with visual timetables that it's important to bear in mind before using them with children:

- We should not assume that the child can read or understand the timetable. This needs to be explicitly taught and explained. Remembering different layouts and symbols impacts understanding.
  - The move from a vertical timetable displayed down the side of the board to a horizontal one going along the bottom of the board may seem immaterial to an adult who is experienced with reading timetables, but not to a child who lacks this knowledge.
  - The move from the daily timetable of a primary school to the weekly, and often two-weekly, timetable at secondary school needs detailed explanation. The simple trick of colour-coding the lessons and matching this to a map of the school, so that, for example, all maths lessons are blue, as are the rooms where they take place on the school map, can be very supportive.

- Some children need support to understand that information in a group timetable applies to them, as they struggle to see themselves as part of that larger group. Some of these children can be supported by a 'name tag' to remind them that it applies to them, but others will need a personalised version of the timetable.

- Not all children will follow the same timetable during the day. For children who are going out for intervention groups, appointments, music lessons and so on, their day will be different and this needs to be acknowledged. A list at the side of the timetable or a simple verbal reminder may be enough, but they may need a personal or group timetable to show this to avoid confusion and anxiety.

- The timetable still only provides a certain level of information about what is going to happen. At 11 o'clock it will be maths, but this does not fully explain what is going to happen in that lesson.

Case study: Ibrahim

Ibrahim was adopted from care at the age of 20 months. His forever family was his seventh placement. He displayed a high level of anxiety and struggled to separate from his mother to come into school. His teachers had a visual timetable for the class and a personalised timetable for Ibrahim. But the obvious had been missed: the teaching role was a job share and there were a variety of TAs working in the class. Ibrahim knew what he was going to do in the classroom, but not who with. So, his teachers made a set of pictures of all the staff who were regularly in the classroom. At the end of each day, Ibrahim worked with an adult to find and display the pictures of the adults who would be in the classroom the next day. While not resolving Ibrahim's difficulties coming into school, it did calm them. It was important for him to have an 'oops card' that could be added to allow for staff absences.

Instead of this...	... try this
You put the visual timetable up by the board and run through it at high speed, naming each subject.	Put the timetable up with the children, perhaps asking one of the children who most needs the support of the timetable to put up the cards. When you are putting up the timetable, add a little information about what will be happening in each lesson: 'In maths, we will be adding two- and three-digit numbers.'

The tips that follow will help you to use visual timetables effectively and overcome some of the problems identified above.

Tip 1: Use an oops card
A timetable set out at the beginning of the day cannot predict the unexpected. This can in part be helped by an 'oops card'.

This can be added to the timetable as necessary to explain a change to plans during the day (for example, PE will be indoors because it is raining) or help children to manage the unexpected (such as a fire drill). It is worth practising with an 'oops card' to get children used to minor and 'safe' changes, so they can build the experience they need to manage a more significant 'oops' when needed. Also, make sure you have some blank cards, so special events can be added and are clear.

Tip 2: Visual does not necessarily mean pictorial
As children become more confident readers, you do not necessarily need a picture or symbol for each part of the timetable. As you move from pictures and symbols to words, the use of colours to indicate different subjects and activities can be helpful and can act as a preparation for a move towards a more complicated written timetable. Also, it marks the fact that break and lunchtime play are similar in expectations.

Tip 3: Plan and prepare for the next day
Consider putting up the timetable for the next day before the children leave, so they know what they will be doing when they return to school in the morning. You will need to go through it again in the morning.

Tip 4: Going home
Don't forget to include a 'home' card, so that it is clear when the day will end and the children will be going home. Also consider those going to after-school clubs and activities.

Support for routines within the lesson

As we have said, some children will need an individual timetable to help them navigate through the day. But all children will benefit from a more detailed breakdown of what will happen in the lesson. We plan the lessons so their structure is clear to us, but this is not clear to the children or often even to the TAs, who are not involved in the planning of the lessons.

As mentioned, it is one thing to know that the lesson will be maths but another to know what is going to happen in the lesson. What topics will be covered? What activities will the child be expected to engage in and what interaction will be needed with others to achieve the expected outcome? What is that outcome and what does it look like? These are all unpredictable. The more we are able to reduce anxieties about these, the greater the chances of children actively engaging in the learning and doing so calmly. This can be supported by going through the lesson expectations and structure before starting the lesson. This should be visual.

Instead of this…	… try this
When the children come into the lesson, you tell them to open their books and copy the date and learning intention from the book. Then you launch into an explanation of the role of ghosts in *Hamlet*, including a brief excursion to describe various productions of the play that you have seen. Then you ask the children to read the scene where Hamlet sees his father's ghost. Then write about it. The majority of the children will have taken the learning intention and translated this to understand what the expected outcome will be. They will have picked the information they need from the various activities to support this. But some will not have been able to apply their knowledge of previous lessons to identify this. Others will misidentify which is the key information as they lack an understanding of the big picture or a 'route map' through it.	The children come into the lesson and you display a flow chart on the board and explain each stage of the lesson and highlight the information they will need to gather from it to complete the final learning activity. A smaller version of the flow chart is shown on each lesson slide, showing the class's progress through the lesson. There is a clear link between the learning intention, what is happening in the lesson and what the children will be expected to do. This is made explicit and visible, so it is more accessible to more children.

There are a number of commonly used structures to help children understand what they need to do within a lesson, which can be used with individuals, groups or even the whole class to support them through the lesson. This is not just a matter of making the lesson structure clear and increasing security within the classroom; it is also about supporting children to remember and follow instructions.

Case study: Fergus

Fergus struggled with transitions. Every PE lesson, he had a meltdown about changing into his PE kit. Both his mum and teacher were clear that he could dress himself and there were no particular sensory issues about the kit. He was not being asked to do anything that he couldn't do easily; however, it was a major issue and barrier to him taking part in the learning. Despite her scepticism because of his skills with dressing and undressing, the teacher agreed to give Fergus visual prompts set out as a flow diagram, showing what clothes to take off, in what order and then the order to put on his PE kit. The meltdowns stopped. He knew what to do when it was quiet and in the safety of his home, but in the bustle of the classroom, he couldn't manage it. He needed a visual prompt to remind him. It took time to create, but it saved time and stress for both Fergus and his teacher.

Things to try

By removing areas of stress by making instructions and routines easier to follow, we free up children's energy, emotion and concentration to cope with the challenges of learning. The following resources may help you to support this.

Visual checklists and instructions can be created for common daily routines, such as collecting belongings at the end of the day or going to lunch. These can be visual or written. For example:

Have you got your
Reading Record?

Have you got
your **bag?**

Have you got
your **PE bag?**

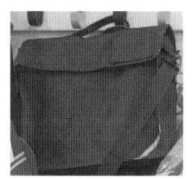

Have you got your
book bag?

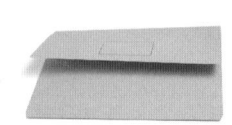

Have you got your **home
learning folder?**

Have you got
your **jumper?**

Now and next cards come in a number of different versions. Commonly, they are used with individuals to reduce uncertainty in their day and make expectations explicit. They show that 'Now' you are doing this and 'Next' you will be doing that. This is depicted using visual prompts or symbols. The cards can be used at different levels to move the child from one lesson to the next (Now: Maths; Next: English) or from one activity to the next within the lesson (for example: Now: Listening to the teacher; Next: Writing one paragraph about our science experiment). For children with issues with engagement or who are displaying a high level of anxiety, it can be helpful to use **if and then cards** instead. For example: 'If you do this [activity chosen by the adult], then you can do [a motivational activity].'

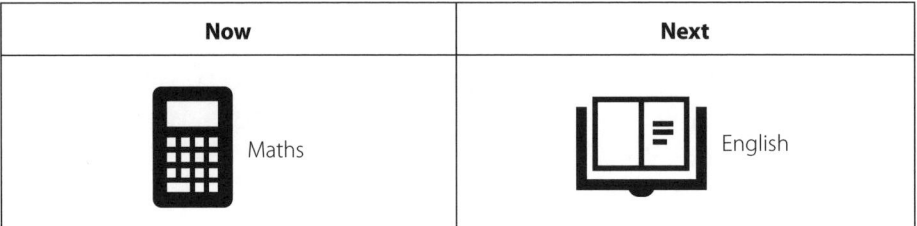

Now	Next
Maths	English

Task-management boards can vary from a simple checklist on a whiteboard to a piece of paper listing what is expected in the lesson, on which the child can tick off each task or activity as it is completed. They are sometimes a more complicated laminated board, for example:

Task:	To be able to use place value apparatus for addition	
Equipment needed: Maths book, pencil, ruler and place value apparatus		
	Job	**Done**
1	Copy the calculation into your book.	✓
2	Match the figures and place value apparatus.	
3	Put all the ones together. If you have more than 10 ones, swap them for tens.	
4	Put all the tens together.	
5	Count the tens. Count the ones. Write the answer.	

You can download a printable copy of a blank task-management board from www.bloomsbury.com/the-inclusive-classroom.

A task-management board enables the child to track their progress through the lesson and works as an aide memoire for what to do next. For many, the simple process of going through the task and identifying the elements involved in it is enough.

Case study: Robert

Robert struggled with self-organisation and managing change. Also, he hated to be made to feel different to his classmates. His SEN support plan said that he should use a task-management board and it was clear without this support that he struggled to remember what to do next. Without this support, he would engage in the first part of any task, usually recording the learning intention and date, and then panic, disrupt and do little. It was difficult to reconcile his two conflicting needs.

It was agreed that once Robert was settled, an adult would sit beside him and a friend, who also benefited from a task-management board, and make a list for each of them of the stages of the activity on a whiteboard. The breaking down and verbalising of this provided an element of support. Robert then slipped his board under his books where it couldn't be seen. Sometimes, he would sneak a look to check that he was doing the right thing, but it was the talking through and breaking down of the task that really made the difference for him and his friend.

Modelled outcomes provide a series of examples that display the steps of a task so that children can follow them, which can be very supportive. For some children, not knowing or understanding the stages of an activity or what the final product should look like can be so paralysing that they are not able or willing to start the task. For example:

Column method

$$
\begin{array}{r}
5\ 6\ 7 \\
1\ 9\ 9\,{}^{+} \\
{}_{1}\ \ {}_{1}\ \ \ \\
\hline
7\ 6\ 6 \\
\end{array}
$$

Early success

Key to enabling and supporting children to engage with learning is to endow them with the confidence that they can and will succeed. There is an old adage that success builds success. Certainly, this is true for children. Therefore, it is essential to lay the foundations of success at the beginning of the lesson, so that you set them up with a feeling of 'I can…'. Where SEN support so often goes wrong is when the teacher has set up a task that they think that the children can do really well, but it goes wrong and children are left feeling like failures.

If we consider our own experiences of trying to set up a new piece of technology, we know that when, as so often happens, it doesn't work, we are left feeling frustrated, angry and a failure. However, we have the life experience to know that the problem can be solved. We can try again. We can ask for help. We have the resilience to move on. Unfortunately, many children lack this, so that even a small setback can establish a pattern and self-belief that they can't.

Therefore, we need to ensure that children are able to succeed with the first steps of their learning, so that they are able to access the next steps. By doing this and building resilience and positive self-talk, we can change their engagement in learning. In many ways this goes beyond the teaching of subject knowledge to the development of the underlying skills that enable children to access learning. However, our attempts to support and develop positive self-esteem and resilience can go from the sublime to ridiculous and false praise. Children are quick to identify this and the sense of being patronised is highly damaging. But simple, achievable first steps and a prompted start can set the pathway for success.

Case study: Hardeep

Hardeep struggled with learning in all areas, but maths was his particular hate. He would refuse to engage. He would begin sitting with his head on the desk, moaning and complaining that he couldn't do it before the task was even introduced. It was clear that something needed to be done to change his view of himself and his learning. After considerable discussion, it was agreed that he would start each maths lesson with a colouring activity. These started as simple activities, for example, colouring by numbers, and then were extended so that he added number bonds to five and then to ten to identify which colour to use to complete the picture. This motivating activity slowly built his confidence and self-belief to begin to tackle the same calculations without the additional motivator. Yet it was still important to start each session with something that Hardeep felt confident with to remind him that he could do maths.

Instead of this...	... try this
Toby has an EHCP, so someone always sits by him in all lessons and prompts and supports him. This builds a belief in Toby and the adults around him that he *must* have an adult to attempt any learning. He has no confidence or resilience to attempt learning independently. He has become prompt-dependent.	Toby has an EHCP. When the work is set for the class, the teacher gives Toby time to settle. Then she sits for a few minutes with him, repeating the instructions and breaking down the task. She then sets him a few simple examples to build his confidence, leaving him to get on with them. Having settled the other children, the teacher returns and checks that Toby is happy and knows what to do. Again, she leaves him to work independently, returning throughout the lesson to check on and celebrate Toby's progress. Toby is prompted for independence.

Top tips for building confidence and self-belief

Key to children's ability to tackle a task is a belief that they can succeed. These are some tips to support children to build that belief and so promote their success.

Tip 1: Staggered start

Rather than making all the children sit through the teacher input even if they are unable to access it, thus building a sense of frustration and failure, start some children with an accessible starter activity – perhaps some pre- or over-learning (see page 60). When the others are settled, you can work with this group in a focused manner.

Tip 2: 'Five and I'll be back'

As the children are settling into their work, ensure that the focus child understands the task. Go over areas of confusion. Then give them time to start the activity with the promise of your return in five minutes. This allows them to attempt the work, but also gives them the reassurance that support will be available if they need it before they become disheartened or frustrated. At the same time, they have the opportunity to develop their resilience to learn independently.

Tip 3: Scaffolding

There is a lot of talk about scaffolding in schools, but little clarity about what it means. This is the process where, through the provision of prompts and carefully directed questions, children are supported to progress through the work while they maintain control. It gives confidence and support with completing the work for the child. Often this can be done by providing a framework or structure for the child to complete by entering their own ideas so that they can focus on the ideas they want to share and explain, rather than how to organise them.

Tip 4: Modelling – sentence starters and worked examples

For many of us, one of the big fears is the blank sheet of paper. By providing a structure for the child to copy or complete, we can reduce this fear without them becoming dependent on an adult scribing and them copying.

Pre- and over-learning

Key to supporting children to access learning is ensuring that they understand what we are talking about, both in terms of the expectations of the lesson and, more fundamentally, in terms of the language and vocabulary we use in the lesson. Pre- and over-learning are the starting points for this.

This approach promotes children staying in the mainstream classroom, is easy to implement and requires neither specialist technology nor equipment. In essence:

- **Pre-learning** is giving the children a heads-up of what will go on in a particular lesson and the ideas and language they will need to access it.

- **Over-learning** is going over the key points with the children again afterwards to embed them.

- This is based on the idea that interventions should:

  ○ be rooted in the actual classroom and on the curriculum material

  ○ be measurable in terms of engagement with the curriculum and participation in the classroom

  ○ not distract from the curriculum but directly foster a more positive engagement with the class material

  ○ boost self-esteem and motivation to learn the curriculum among peers in the classroom.

Imagine that the children are studying volcanoes and an identified child is removed from this lesson to practise reading about Billy the Goat. After a term, the teacher notices that the student's reading comprehension age has risen, yet he knows nothing about the difference between magma and lava and still doesn't volunteer to read because he is only confident when studying in the corridor with his TA. This is not supporting his learning or engagement in the classroom.

Pre- and over-learning work to support children with a range of SEN needs. There is considerable evidence (see Bergland, 2014) that deficits in language and vocabulary have the greatest impact on children from disadvantaged backgrounds. In a paper in *Nature Neuroscience* (Shibata et al., 2017), researchers found that even brief periods (up to 20 minutes) of over-learning after a task led to improved performance. This occurred because the over-learning resulted in a more stable neural state, which was less prone to disruption by the arrival of new information. In other words, putting new stuff in your brain can lead to dumping other information to make space, but over-learning helps it feel more at home. An implication of this is that simply coming back to a task a few times later on can enable the teacher to be sure that what could have been an initially errorless performance by the learner was genuinely the result of mastery, and not just a one-off. In addition, as information fades after a month or so, over-learning needs to be combined with semi-regular spaced practice for the optimal retention of skills and knowledge; in other words, teachers should revisit topics every month, rather than revise them only prior to tests or exams at the end of the year.

Pre-learning can set up the condition where the main lesson actually becomes a period of over-learning. The same cognitive and neural mechanisms that support over-learning during a lesson therefore also support the efficacy of pre-learning. This may be especially useful for learners with low prior knowledge, students with poor working memory or those with any SEN.

> *I was in two secondary schools in the same week. They were both studying* Frankenstein *in English lessons. The first school had invested £20,000 in a computer-based learning programme. Children who had reading comprehension challenges were withdrawn from the English class to spend a session using the programme. Their comprehension skills increased somewhat, and it was a very focused way to do this. In the other school these children were not withdrawn. A TA sat with them at the beginning of the lesson and told them what was coming up in the lesson: the key points, where they were up to in the story of Frankenstein, the key words they would learn, the key questions and some of the answers, which they could use to participate. At the end of the lesson, the TA went back over these points with the children. The impact was that the children who had done the pre- and over-learning were able to participate in the class and their progress within the curriculum itself was significant. Not only that, but their self-esteem for learning, their interest in reading and their sense of belonging also grew. In the first school, the children's specific skill of reading comprehension increased but their curriculum engagement decreased. They didn't make any particular progress in their learning behaviours across the year or in their sense of belonging in the school.*
>
> *Daniel*

Pre-learning and over-learning are very clever and effective interventions and 99 per cent of all children will be supported by them, enabling them to be able to engage effectively in the classroom. The impact on behaviour is radical because it's showing children that they are cared for and noticed. The beauty of the intervention is that it doesn't cost anything, it's easy to implement and it gets right to the jugular of core challenges. It's also very trackable and visible. You can offer children an answer to give in advance and then their peers can turn around and be impressed that they answered a question. Suddenly, they feel like school is a successful experience.

Instead of this...	... try this
It is maths. You need to get started so you introduce a quick warm-up and then head into the main body of the lesson. Time is of the essence and assessments are next week. As the lesson goes on, it becomes clear that many of the children are unsure of what is going on and several have significant misconceptions. You have to stop the class and unravel the misconceptions. By the end of the lesson, you are rushed and stressed and haven't covered the content needed for the assessments.	You spend a few minutes of over-learning, revisiting the key concepts from the last lesson. It becomes clear that there are several misconceptions. You tackle these with the whole class. Then you use pre-learning to introduce the key vocabulary needed for the lesson, providing visual prompts to help the children to remember it. Once the majority of the class are settled, you work with the group still struggling with the content from yesterday. By the end of the lesson, the learning is on track and you are ready for next week.

Top tips for pre- and over-learning

The following tips are designed to help you to use pre-learning and over-learning effectively in the classroom.

- Use pre- and over-learning in the classroom rather than outside the classroom.

- Focus on skills and ideas rather than just key words. Get children to draw or source a picture of the new word or relate it to a story. Abstract words are tough for anyone. Some children may benefit from creating their own visual dictionary.

- Use each task as a framework for teacher–TA liaison: include structures of forthcoming lessons and details about how identified children are acquiring new language and engaging with the topic.

- Use pre-learning as a hook for a new topic and to motivate children to want to discover more. Motivation and engagement go together. Fun, excitement, mystery and linking to favourite icons and heroes can help.

- You don't have to but try using technology: record sentences on devices that can be used during lesson time. Videos and audio can all help with language acquisition.

- Homework is an over-learning opportunity if designed properly. This is another topic in itself but be careful about introducing new ideas just because you are desperately trying to finish the topic in time.

- Initial pre-learning should ideally be done twice – once every couple of weeks in advance and again just prior to the lesson.

- Over-learning should be done after the lesson and again every few weeks. Keep coming back to the learning; don't let it drop until two weeks before the end-of-year assessments.

Summary

'Start as you mean to go on' is one of the nice-sounding phrases that everyone would keenly give a nod of agreement to. It's actually more nuanced than it may initially appear. We hope that we have given enough considerations to think through the potential danger points and you now have a list of top tips from which to choose a few to try out. Use the table below as an action plan to prompt you *if* you have the time and you find this kind of summary useful.

Identified issue	Suggestion/Check	My action	Any impact?
Considering the room	Physical, sensory, visual and auditory		
	Sitting comfortably		
	Seating plans		
	Supporting focus		
Supporting routines	Predictability		
	Anxiety-free routines		
Feeling early successes	Building confidence and self-belief		
	Pre-learning		
Greeting	Warmth and encouragement		
	Clarity of positive expectations		
	Staggered starts or entry		

2 Phase 2 of the lesson: Whole-class engagement: delivering and receiving instructions

'We need to enable the development of communication and language skills in children by creating lots of small opportunities to clarify our meaning. Effective engagement can then lead to real progress. We have to be really aware of how much our communication can either include or alienate all of our children, especially the most challenging and vulnerable.' Sara Alston

Once we have got the children safely and effectively into the classroom, the next step is almost always the delivering of instructions – what to do – or instruction – what we are learning about. For either of these to be effective, we need to maximise the communication and the children's engagement. This is the focus of this phase of the lesson.

The successful delivery and communication of instructions depends both on the skills of the teacher and their listeners. Often children's ability to listen to and understand what is said to them is inhibited by difficulties with hearing, focus and attention, speech and language difficulties or even difficulties based on the fact they and the teacher do not share a common language. The child and the teacher may literally not have a language in common or they may both be speaking English but lack the shared, and sometimes technical and subject-specific, vocabulary to support mutual understanding. Furthermore, the physical act of hearing and the interpretation of what has been said are different. An awareness of the fact that what you say may not be the same as what is understood or perceived is the key starting point to support the effective delivery of instructions in the classroom.

How to ensure that the message you communicate is understood

Case study: Donnie

Donnie is very literal in his understanding of everything. The teacher may say to the class, 'Write the date and the learning intention.' While most pupils would do this and then get on with the task, Donnie would write the date and the learning intention and then just sit quietly. As far as he could tell, he had followed the instructions and done as he was told. The rest of the children could infer the implied instruction to then get on with the learning task; Donnie could not.

Most people today know that effective communication between two people is far more than just verbal. The 'talk' bit is a tiny proportion of how a message is articulated and received. In fact, as much as 93 per cent of our communication is non-verbal (Mehrabian, 1972), as represented in the pie chart below. The very idea that our species has evolved an ability to communicate in specific and nuanced detail is perhaps one of our foundational cornerstones. With this in mind, one of the primary outcomes of any good education system must be to enable its students to communicate clearly, thoughtfully and with confidence across a range of topics and scenarios. A child's ability to understand *and* to be understood is paramount for good mental health and socialisation (see No Isolation, 2017; I CAN Help; Royal College of Speech and Language Therapists, 2019). In essence, a large part of what we are teaching is communication, both verbal and non-verbal. In addition, just as the outcome is critical, the use of good communication *during* teaching is also vital.

Albert Mehrabian devised the 7-38-55 communication rule, which suggests that the way we interpret a message is 7% verbal, 38% vocal and 55% non-verbal.

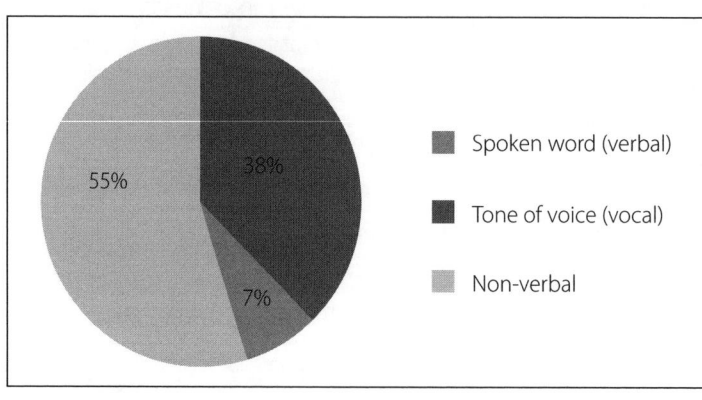

It's not what you say, it's the way that you say it

Plenty of us who appeared busy at school didn't actually learn very much. Most challenging behaviours are rooted in misunderstanding instructions and the unwritten codes around how to participate in learning and school life. Responding to behaviours is too often about managing the behaviour itself rather than considering the antecedents and causes. Often, the major issues that go unchecked arise from situations where children simply haven't understood what the teacher asked them to do, so they do something else or nothing at all. This is then mistakenly perceived as misbehaviour or laziness.

The following communication shows how a simple message can be lost on some children:

> *A teacher says: 'Wait a minute.'*
>
> *The teacher means: 'I will be with you shortly, but I must do something else prior to giving you my attention.'*
>
> *Most children will perceive this to mean: 'The teacher will pay me attention when they have finished what they're doing, and I can wait until then.' They are able to wait without anxiety.*
>
> *A child with literal understanding may perceive this to mean: 'I need to wait 60 seconds, no more and no less.'*
>
> *A child who has experienced trauma may perceive this to mean: 'I don't like you and I don't want to deal with you ever.'*

Each child in this scenario may then respond to the message as they have perceived it. As a teacher, it's not *what* you communicate or even necessarily *how*: it's entirely about what is perceived or understood.

In such cases, either the adult gets cross and the child feels angry or embarrassed and shows this through 'poor behaviour', or the child realises that they have got it wrong and feels stupid or upset and shows this through 'poor behaviour'. Either way, the adult sees and responds to the behaviour, rather than addressing the misunderstandings caused by a failure of communication.

It's worth noting the desperately sad truth underlying the high incidents of language and communication problems found in prison inmates (Bryan et al., 2007), which suggests at least a correlation, if not a direct cause and effect, between people who can't function well in society and their ability to understand and be understood. It's not a far stretch to think of this as being a major cause of disruptive behaviours in the micro-society of the classroom.

It's surprising, then, that we don't include the development of communication skills in any great detail in teacher training or in the curriculum beyond Early Years. The Early Years Foundation Profile (Standards and Testing Agency, 2020) includes communication and language development as one of its prime areas of development. To achieve a 'good level of development', children need to develop their skills for:

- listening and attention
- understanding and speaking, including awareness of the needs of the listener.

However, the entire speaking and listening curriculum for Key Stages 1 *and* 2 consists of a mere 12 bullet points, and while children need to be able to gain, maintain and monitor the interest of their listeners, they do not need to consider whether they have understood *what* they are saying. By Key Stage 3, spoken language is given a single eight-line paragraph (Department for Education, 2013). This is clearly insufficient. Children have not learned all they need to learn about communication and language development, particularly the key skills of making sure that they have been understood, by the age of five. In addition, we should recognise that the skills of making oneself understood and being aware of whether we have been successfully understood are crucial for effective teaching. The efficacy of communication by children (and adults) is assumed to be achieved as a by-product of our curriculum-based activities but not the ultimate goal. At the very least, we should prioritise and monitor this aspect of learning for the most vulnerable and challenging children throughout their school lives.

Communication skills are the foundation for all learning. Children learn communication skills not in one specific lesson but in every lesson, and of course, not just in lessons; the front desk, the dining hall and every human encounter is a lesson in how to communicate. This also includes all the terrible habits and negative messages that can damage a child's sense of worth and self-perception. Indeed, managing interactions successfully at playtime and lunchtime depends on these untaught skills. Those of us who regularly work with children who are diagnosed as being on the autistic spectrum are aware that implicit communication skills need to be taught explicitly to those children, but this can mask the need to teach them to *all* children. This is a good example of how the 'label' can eclipse the very same need in children without a label.

The need for clear communication is by no means restricted to a specific part of a lesson, but it is most felt at the point when the teacher has dispensed with the introductions and gives the instruction to 'begin the task', be it a physical activity or writing or indeed any activity. At some point in almost every lesson, the teacher will need a child to 'do something' – and, yes, this even includes watching a film.

These are some of the common behaviours that children may exhibit to mask their misunderstanding, which they may or may not be conscious of:

- confidently answer or do something other than what the teacher asked, whether it is a different task or the right task but in completely the wrong way
- confidently write a small amount, convinced that they have fully and perfectly answered the question

- tentatively answer something in a brief way because they don't feel sure they are doing the right thing

- be quietly busy and engaged in something, including 'helping' someone else, that at a quick glance looks like completing the task but, in reality, is not

- procrastinate but appear to be trying hard; inside, they feel anxious and lost in the lesson, but they don't want to attract the attention of the teacher or get into trouble

- avoid engaging with the task because they have no idea what to do; they may appear to be messing around and not settling in small and annoying ways, or perform a big behaviour to distract from the task at hand, such as get into a confrontation or feign sickness.

When the child's masking of their lack of understanding is not a big and disruptive behaviour, it is very easy to assume that they understand.

Case study: Simmie

Simmie was quiet in class but seemed to perform well. He always tried to sit at the front of the class, which made him appear enthusiastic but meant that he was not in the teacher's eyeline as they scanned the room. He always put his hand up, so the teacher assumed he knew the answer. If he was called on, Simmie would mumble, and as his speech wasn't very clear, the teacher would often just agree and move on rather than push him to explain. When given a task, Simmie would get on busily and appear to be engaged. It was only when you actually focused on what Simmie was doing that it became clear that he had no idea what was happening in class. In fact, his book was full of random words and phrases he had copied from the classroom walls. Like so many of us when we don't understand, Simmie had covered up and masked, but he had done it quietly, looking busy and engaged, so his teachers assumed that he had understood.

It is hard to admit that you don't understand, and even harder once you have started on a course of action to admit that you were wrong. Given that this is hard for adults (present company included), it is significantly more so for children. There are some children who will put up their hand and ask for help, and some who will be able to say, 'I don't understand,' but often they are not clear what it is that they don't understand. In the busy classroom, it is easier to say, 'Read it again,' or repeat the instruction rather than attempting to get to the root of the misunderstanding. This leaves the child feeling ashamed and embarrassed. It also teaches them not to ask for help.

In other cases, children may show their difficulties with understanding through 'big' actions and disruptive behaviour. We have all come across the 'table-throwers' and those who storm out of the classroom. But, as we have discussed previously, the adult response in school usually focuses on the action, not the communication. Often, we ask, 'Why did you…?' But to explain their behaviour requires more language and self-awareness than the child may possess, particularly when asked while still in a state of heightened emotion and anxiety, which is often the case.

Case study: Tina

Tina is an exceptionally bright 11-year-old: her IQ is on the 99th centile. However, she lives in a constant state of high anxiety. She is terrified that she won't understand and that she won't be the best at everything she does. This anxiety can sometimes cloud her ability to see the simpler and more obvious messages that her teachers are trying to convey. She is terrified of getting things wrong, admitting that she hasn't understood or feeling the shame of 'appearing stupid' in others' judgement. Subconsciously, she would prefer to be thought of as naughty and rebellious. Therefore, she regularly throws objects, kicks, bites and spits rather than risk appearing uncertain. Though she has the language to understand, her *fear* of not understanding is so overwhelming that she *can't* understand. Being asked to explain what she has done and why just serves to heighten her anxiety, adding shame and embarrassment and often leading to another round of explosive behaviour. Even though she has the competence, Tina needs to be supported to manage her fear of failure, and the language needs to be supported by visuals. Her behaviour is an accurate portrayal of her feelings, which she needs help expressing more appropriately in order to be able to progress with the task at hand.

At this point, we would like to make it clear that the subject of speech and language reaches far beyond the scope of this book. Ideally, every teacher in the world would be trained in the fundamentals of speech and language, and we would urge you to invest in books and other resources to learn more about the topic. Effective communication is the very foundation of inclusive teaching. Given the limitations of this book, and perhaps your time, we have chosen to focus on the basics and some skills to practise in a time-friendly way.

Top tips for giving effective instructions

Once you have garnered the children's attention (see the previous chapters for our thoughts and ideas about how to do this), it is important to make sure that you are giving your instructions as effectively as possible. The following tips will help to support you with this.

Tip 1: Avoid giving too many instructions at a time

We are amazed by the number of teachers who tell us that a child in their class can only manage instructions with two or three information-carrying words (ICWs) and yet expect them to follow instructions with four or more ICWs. It is important that our communications are clear and coherent for children. If they can't understand or remember what we say, they can't possibly do what we have asked of them.

An information-carrying word (ICW) is a word that carries meaning. If language is supported by gestures and visuals, there may be no ICWs in an instruction. Let's take as an example: 'Give me the toy car.' Here, the words in the instruction that the child needs to understand can be reduced if you are sitting at a table with a toy car on it; you can look at the toy and hold out your hand. However, if you don't look at the car, this becomes a one-ICW instruction. If the child is asked to 'put the car on the table', there are two words they need to understand. The child can be expected to understand 'put', 'the' and 'on' from their previous experience.

Tip 2: Support your instructions with gestures and facial expressions

As we highlighted at the beginning of the chapter, only a tiny percentage of our communication is verbal. To make our communication as effective as possible in the classroom, we need to consciously utilise body language and gestures to support and reinforce our message. This can range from simply pointing to where we want a child to move to or at the object we want them to pick up, to the use of a raised hand to indicate 'stop' or an upwards gesture to indicate that you want the children to stand up. There are more complex ways of using 'sign language' with your class to share meaning. Many teachers develop this with their class to support both class routines and learning.

Remember that if your body language is communicating one thing while you are saying something else, the children will become confused and the message will not get across.

Consider the safety briefing on an aeroplane: the cabin crew speak, they direct your attention to where the exits are and how to use the life-saving equipment, and then they advise you to read the safety card in the pocket in front of you. This is life-saving information, and so it is offered to passengers in three different ways to maximise the chances that it can be understood. How can we emulate this in the classroom?

Case study: Sadie

Sadie struggles to read and understand facial expressions, so it is important that these are highlighted and explained to her to build her understanding and support effective communication. When her teachers are pleased with her, they say, 'Sadie, I am happy with you. Look at my face [pointing to their face]. I am smiling, and that means I am happy.' The repeated use of this script and explicitly directing Sadie to look at their facial expressions slowly builds her understanding of this simple non-verbal communication.

A child like Sadie, who cannot recognise facial expressions, may well be referred for an appointment at CAMHS; however, it could take up to 12 months just to be seen, and then an additional six months before they meet once with a psychiatric nurse. This will not solve the issue. It might give a diagnosis, but it will not change the child's needs. Communication is what we learn from the adults around us and supporting this is one thing that all teachers can do that requires no extra time, money or stress, but that will make a remarkable difference to both the teachers and their pupils.

With the pressures and demands of teaching, we can find ourselves giving half-instructions or even depending on implied instructions. Perhaps when we say: 'Get your book,' we actually want the children to infer, 'Get your book, open it and get on with your work.' It can be a challenge to constantly support our instructions with visual prompts when there are so many competing needs and events going on in the classroom.

Instead of this...	... try this
The class teacher asks three children to line up by the door. She looks at her list to confirm who are the chosen children and rattles off their names without looking up. The children are not supported to know to whom she is giving the instruction. Some have heard a name and have responded, so both Eva and Evie have joined the queue in the belief that they were called. Three random children who heard the number three and were keen to get involved are also in the line. Meanwhile two of the children who needed to join the line haven't as they didn't understand what to do.	The class teacher asks three children to line up by the door. As she says 'three', she holds up three fingers. Then as she names the children, she points to them in turn and makes eye contact. In this way, a simple and quick solution gives clarity to the whole class.

Tip 3: Provide written instructions

We all know that it is easier to remember things when they are written down. This is why we spend our time writing to-do lists. Yet often we expect children to remember long verbal lists of instructions. Children can't follow instructions if they don't remember them, so it is important to make these as easy to remember as possible.

Be aware of your language:

- A long and detailed instruction is probably not going to be followed.

- Be careful not to cause problems with children who take instructions literally, even though you know that most children would understand nuanced differences in wording, for example, asking children to pull their socks up.

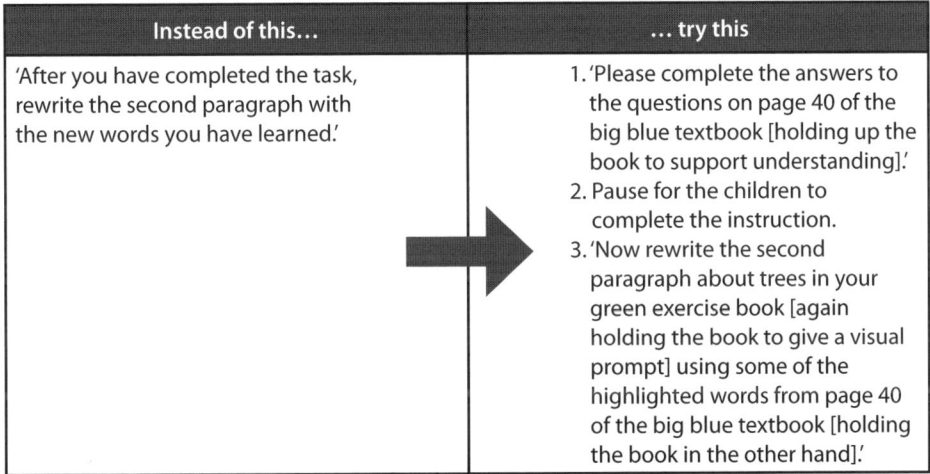

Instead of this...	... try this
'After you have completed the task, rewrite the second paragraph with the new words you have learned.'	1. 'Please complete the answers to the questions on page 40 of the big blue textbook [holding up the book to support understanding].' 2. Pause for the children to complete the instruction. 3. 'Now rewrite the second paragraph about trees in your green exercise book [again holding the book to give a visual prompt] using some of the highlighted words from page 40 of the big blue textbook [holding the book in the other hand].'

Tip 4: Use visuals and symbols to support your instructions

It is worth building up a bank of visuals to use for regular instructions, such as a picture of a book for 'Get your book out.' Most children find it easier to follow visual instructions, rather than either written or verbal instructions. This reduces the number of ICWs they need to understand and remember.

You might display instructions on your board. See below and on page 74 for some examples.

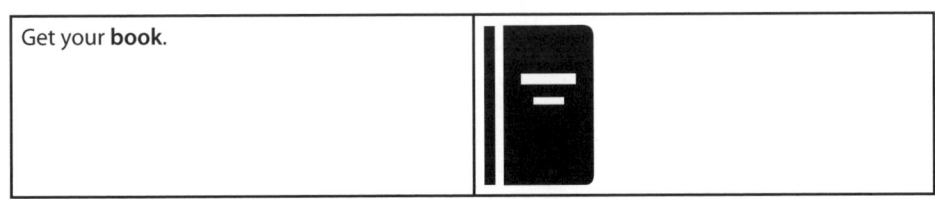

Get your **book**.

Get your **pencil**.	
Look at the **board**, ready to start your work.	

Some children will need a personalised list or series of visuals. Some will benefit from a laminated list on which they can tick off tasks as they are completed. This both reduces anxiety and clarifies the communication for the teacher as well as the child.

Tip 5: Avoid making instructions overly complicated

Once we have made sure the information-carrying words are of a level the children can follow and they are supported by modelling, visuals and effective gestures and body language, we need to think about *what* we are in fact asking children to do. All too often we add additional instructions to an activity that is already in progress, making the task increasingly complex. For example:

'Everyone get your books.'
The children shuffle around to get their books.
[Loudly] 'And pick up a worksheet from the front desk.'
Most children start moving to the front, when the teacher realises that glue sticks are needed.
[Loudly] 'And grab a glue stick from the red drawer at the back.'

Many children will not be able to keep up with these changes.

We often further complicate things by mixing instructions intended for different groups.

Instead of this...	... try this
'Red group, get your book, but those who haven't finished the work from yesterday need to complete that task first. By the way, John, you were away and need to complete the work from yesterday so you should work with Ms Brown. Yellow group need to pick up the blue sheets from the front. Blue group need to collect three yellow stickers from the back.'	While pointing to the symbol for the Red group say: 'Red group [then wait until they are looking]: if you haven't finished yesterday's work about lemons then do that.' Count the tasks off on your fingers. Pause and let them start to move. Then 'name tag' John, check that he is listening and say: 'John, you need to work with Ms Brown as you were away yesterday.'

By separating the instructions for each group or for key individuals and ensuring that they are all following them before addressing the next group, we maximise the chances that our instructions can be understood and followed.

As teachers, we feel so much pressure to get things done and are so used to thinking on our feet that we forget that doing this can make it harder for others to follow what we are talking about. Clear communication with our class includes planning what we want to say before we say it.

Tip 6: Avoid confusing instructions and chat

For many children, teachers' chatty and humorous asides are an important part of building relationships. However, for many, particularly those with social communication or speech and language difficulties, this general chatter becomes very confusing when muddled with instructions. These children can struggle to differentiate between the two. Try to keep your instructions and general chat separate so that you are modelling both clear instructions and how to share general conversation.

Instead of this...	... try this
'I used to know someone who studied geography and he actually visited a volcano and he showed me his photos. They were amazing and you could see actual lava spurting out. So, I'd like you to draw a volcano with lots of hot lava coming out. He told me that the volcano was particularly hot and quite stinky because of the sulphur smelling like farts. OK, so get on and draw please.'	Tell the great story about your friend who visited the volcano; give a clear pause and then move on: 'This is the task we are going to do now: draw a volcano with lava running down the side.' At the same time, show them a picture of a volcano and display the instructions on the board.

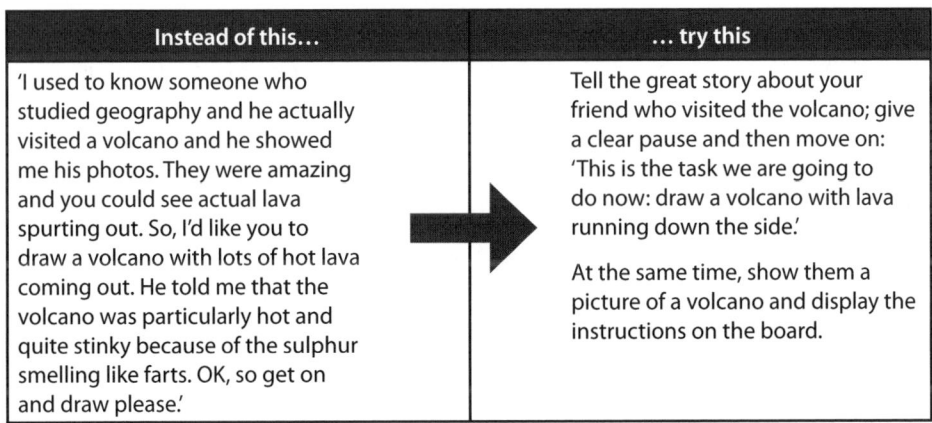

Tip 7: Avoid repeating the same instruction in different ways

As teachers, we do this all the time. We say, 'Get your English book' and then when the child hasn't done it, we add, 'Pick up your blue book.' If a child is struggling to process language, giving the same instruction in different ways may increase their confusion. We also need to be aware that TAs often repeat teachers' instructions. Their well-meaning attempts to simplify language can inadvertently add to the confusion as the child tries to process several sets of instructions and establish whether they are the same or different, as well as trying to work out what they mean and what action they require. Often, this results in the child doing nothing at all as their energy is focused on deciphering this verbal puzzle. Then they are told off for not following the instructions.

Instead of this...	... try this
'Get what you need to start your learning. You'll need your book. Your green maths book. Sean, check you have the right book please.' Shortly afterwards you see that some children haven't followed your instruction, so you add: 'Green book, maths book. You all need your green maths book, now! Hurry up, we need to get on.'	'Get your green maths book.' Point to a green maths book, ideally Sean's, so that you can give it straight to him. Say it once and wait for the children to follow the instruction. If needed, repeat the same instruction in the same way.

Case study: Michael

Five-year-old Michael's teacher was getting increasingly fed up that he never helped with tidying up. She would put on the 'tidy up music' – the class-taught routine – and the other children would dart happily around the room, collecting resources, picking up rubbish and setting out the yellow 'Don't Touch – Learning Continuing' signs. Meanwhile, Michael would pick up one piece of paper and then wander around the room sucking his fingers. Repeated instructions to 'tidy up' meant that again he would collect a single piece of paper and then wander aimlessly. It became clear that Michael had misunderstood what 'tidying up' meant. For him it was just picking up a piece of paper. He also lacked the social understanding to follow the other children's example of what to do, while the 'tidy up music' caused him sensory overload, adding to his anxiety and confusion. In order for Michael to engage in tidying up, he needed specific, modelled tasks.

How to utilise questions effectively and avoid confusion

A good way to become aware of a child's learning process is noticing which questions they ask to clarify, extend and check their understanding. It is assumed that the teacher will ask, and it is perhaps one of the top five job descriptions of any teaching position: ask lots of questions! However, our desire to ask can get in the way of listening to how a child processes their learning.

The teacher asks

All teachers are aware of the need to alter their questions and questioning style to elicit the best responses from different children in their class. It is now generally accepted that 'hands up' allows those who do not put up their hands to opt out, confident that they won't be called on to communicate directly with the teacher, unless they draw attention to themselves in other ways. Alternatively, some children will wave their hand 'confidently' and hope that their enthusiasm will mask their uncertainty and they won't be asked. This has challenged us to find other ways to select children to respond to our questions. There is much of value in the use of various 'randomisers', including tools such as lolly sticks and computer programmes, so that teachers pick, or appear to pick, children at random to answer their question, rather than just call on those with their hands up.

However, for many children, the sudden demand to articulate an idea in front of an audience of their peers is intimidating and highly challenging. Much can be done to alleviate these issues by the careful choice of questions:

- Choose the child before the question so that you don't end up asking the child with an EHCP for moderate learning difficulties to explain a highly complex calculation.

- Use directed and focused questions so that the question is matched to the child's ability and interest. We are advised in teacher training to use open questions. However, for the shy child you are trying to encourage to speak, a closed question may be more effective.

- Many children (and indeed adults) need time to think and formulate their ideas before they can share them in public. This can be supported by a pre-warning of the questions. Let the child know the question and that you will come to them next, so they have time to think and plan their answer.

- Some children will need a further level of support of working with an adult (or peer) to plan their answer verbally. They may benefit from an oral rehearsal of their ideas. They may have the ideas but need the support of others to form them into a coherent sentence that can be shared with the class.

Instead of this...	... try this
You ask multi-stage, open-ended questions. The computer programme you use to randomly select a child to answer the question selects Maria, who is very quiet and shy. Maria turns red, stutters and bursts into tears. You are left with the choice of comforting her and disrupting the lesson or moving on. In neither scenario does Maria answer the question.	You decide that you want Maria to share an idea with the class. You gently forewarn her that you are going to ask about a particular subject as she comes into the room, giving her time to prepare an answer. When the time for the question comes, you ask Maria a simple yes/no question. When she has successfully answered, you scaffold a series of single-stage responses, enabling her to gain confidence and share ideas with the class.

The child asks

All teachers will say that they love children asking questions, but in our heart of hearts we know that there are limits to this love. We don't want to be interrupted; we don't want to be asked something that is off subject or, even worse, a question to which we don't know the answer. There may also be a hidden agenda in how we respond to questions. A quick or sarcastic put-down gives a clear message about a teacher's attitude, not only to a question but also to the questioner.

The challenge is to get through the material we need to cover and stay on-topic while enabling children to check their understanding and add to their general learning. The way we manage this is key to good teaching and learning.

> *I was at a local authority briefing. The Director of Education encouraged us to ask questions, and reassured us there was no such thing as a stupid question, but it was said in a manner that made it quite clear he wanted to deliver his message and get out of there as fast as possible. He launched into a presentation heaving with acronyms and abbreviations, which we were all recording with the intention of looking them up later. When a newly appointed headteacher put up her hand and asked for an explanation of one of these, the Director of Education snarled and asked sarcastically who else was 'unaware of the meaning'. Slowly, over 90 per cent of the room, including a brave soul sharing the platform, put up their hands. During the rest of the briefing a number of people raised their hands and asked questions. On the way out, the headteacher was congratulated by colleagues on her bravery for asking the original question.*
>
> *Sara*

Imagine how different the above scenario would have been if the rest of the audience had been aware of the meaning and had not supported the new headteacher. The non-verbal communication at this meeting made it clear that questions were not welcome and that anyone daring to ask one was putting themselves at risk. We need to work to ensure that this is not the message we are subconsciously delivering in our classroom, whether about certain types of questions or about certain questioners.

Instead of this...	... try this
You finish delivering the lesson input and turn quickly to the class, as you gather the exercise books to give out and ask whether there are any questions. Without pausing, you ask a child to give out the books.	Throughout the lesson input, you regularly stop and ask the children to 'dial' with their thumbs to show their confidence with the information. This allows you to ask questions that enable those who are confident to share their understanding, and direct questions at the less confident to explore their understanding.

Here are some ideas to support children to ask questions and for teachers to assess understanding:

- Use thumb dials to ask about confidence and understanding. Children 'dial' their thumbs from thumbs down for 'no idea' through to thumbs up for 'fully confident'.

- Use yes/no cards for children to show their confidence and respond to closed questions.

- Provide opportunities for children to ask questions in private or smaller groups. For example, as a class routine ask children to stay on the carpet or come to the front at the beginning of individual activities if they want to ask or check anything.

- If you have a class of confident writers, have a board where they can record questions or add sticky notes with questions, either anonymously for you to discuss with the whole class or named so you can follow up with the individual.

- Ask each pair or group to explain what they have learned to each other and then ask whether the pair or group have any questions. If you are lucky enough to have an adult working with you, they can support and model this process. This gives an invaluable opportunity to eavesdrop on conversations and assess understanding.

- At the beginning of the lesson, share a list of questions you hope the children will be able to answer by the end of the input.

- Use sentence stems to help children frame and develop questions.

How to encourage participation in learning

'Just because you have communicated doesn't mean the message arrived.' Sara Alston

For children to participate actively and effectively in learning, we need to ensure that they have the skills and opportunities to communicate their learning. This depends on our collective communication being as effective as possible.

Part of the teacher's communication, including our response to their questions, must incorporate a clear message to the children that they can 'understand, take part in and succeed in' learning. In a blog post in 2014, Dylan Wiliam, Emeritus Professor of Educational Assessment at the UCL Institute of Education, wrote:

'If you're not confident or think that you might actually fail when other people will succeed, you will disengage and basically, you will decide that you would rather be thought lazy than stupid.'

The message of 'you can' needs to be given in the context of feedback, but it also needs to be given up front when the instructions and input are being shared. If the instructions are unclear and inaccessible or if you fail to give the child the confidence that they can understand the task and know what to do, they will disengage because it feels safer to be thought of as 'lazy' rather than 'stupid'. For many, the risks of failure are so high that they would prefer not to try: if you don't try, you can't fail. It is part of self-protection for children who are not sure what to do or who may be lacking in confidence that they can succeed with their learning. If we are able to clearly communicate our instructions and expectations and build children's confidence that they *can* succeed, they are more likely to be willing and able to engage in learning. As we have discussed, the classroom needs to be a safe place to ask questions and to admit to not knowing. Moreover, it needs to be a safe place to take risks with learning. In order to support children to feel confident to engage and try learning, we need to ensure that what we are asking of them is within their capabilities.

Case study: Reception class learning to count

The teacher of a Reception class wanted to make good use of the time while two children took the register to the office. She didn't want to start her input without them, so she said that the class would count and see how long it took them to get to the office and back. However, to make it more 'fun', the teacher decided that the children should clap as well as count to keep the rhythm going. It quickly became clear that this additional 'fun' element was adding a level of difficulty that made the task overwhelming. Both clapping in a rhythm and counting required a considerable degree of cognitive challenge for many children in the class. While the majority valiantly tried to engage, many opted out and neither clapped nor counted. A few who were aware that they had been asked to do something that was beyond them started to act out, poking other children, rolling on the carpet or calling out random numbers to distract their classmates.

In this case, some of the children could follow and access the activity, but for others it was too much, and they either opted out or disrupted. We need to consider what additional support is required to make the task accessible for these children. We will look at scaffolding in more detail in the next chapter, but this needs to occur during the input as well as during the completion of activities.

Instead of this...	... try this
When you look at the children's work at the end of the lesson, it becomes clear that many of the children have a number of significant misconceptions. In your plan you have designated the next lesson for covering the next stage of the learning, so that's what you do. In that next lesson, you push ahead with the learning, but the children are increasingly confused and not succeeding, and several are communicating this through 'poor behaviour'.	When you look at the children's work at the end of the lesson, it becomes clear that many of the children have a number of significant misconceptions. As a result, you adapt your planning for the next lesson and revisit the topic using the common misconceptions as a starting point for your teaching. The majority of children are able to understand the learning and you can move on to the next step successfully. There are a few children who are still confused, and you work with them in a focused group to develop their understanding. There is no disruption to the lesson.

Top tips for encouraging participation in learning

For children to make academic and social progress in lessons, the first step is to be willing and able to take part. We have selected a few key things to consider in supporting children's engagement and participation.

1. For some, it is simply a practical issue that the learning information is physically too far away. Often the key points of teaching and useful examples are displayed on a board, but the board is often some metres from the child and there are too many distractions between the child and the board. Simply giving them a personal copy of your PowerPoint slides, so they can mark this text as they move through it, can help.

2. Think about how much you are asking the children to do at a time. Check that your instructions are clear and accessible.

3. Use your seating plan to ensure children are sitting in a place in the class that supports their learning.

4. Use talk partners, pairs and small groups for discussion so that children can benefit from peer support for their learning and a chance to understand how others are approaching tasks. Often, knowing that they are not the only ones who find something difficult will give children the support and confidence to try.

There may be some children who appear all too eager to join in the learning, to the extent that they disrupt others and do not allow them to participate. Indeed, they are so eager that they are constantly shouting out and interrupting the learning of others, and the teacher might need to try a different approach.

Case study: Asha

Asha is very bright and self-confident, though she possesses little awareness of others and their needs. She works out answers quickly and then shouts them across the room at the teacher. This means that others don't have the opportunity to answer or even attempt to work the answer out. This has a significant impact on the rest of the children's learning and the teacher's blood pressure. It was agreed that Asha should sit next to the TA and whisper the answer to her as soon as she had worked it out. Asha was happy to do this and confided in the TA that she had to say it quickly or she forgot her idea. Given this piece of information, Asha was provided with an individual whiteboard to record her ideas and answers so that she didn't forget them. This reduced her disruptive behaviour and built her confidence that she could remember. It stopped her shouting out the answer and increased the engagement of other children as they now felt there was an opportunity to try to answer the teacher's questions.

Instead of this...	... try this
Alfie constantly shouts out and each lesson becomes a battle of wills between him and the teacher to see who can share more information about the learning. The rest of the class sits in confusion, and the teacher becomes increasingly frustrated and stressed.	At the beginning of the lesson, Alfie is told that he can share three points during the lesson, and he is given a card to represent each one. He is warned to use them carefully – if he goes over his allocation, he will be allowed to share fewer points in future lessons. He is given a set of the lesson slides, so that he can begin to plan when he wants to share his points, and a whiteboard to record his ideas on. Each time Alfie shares an idea, he is reminded of the points he still has to share. It takes time, but slowly Alfie becomes more able to wait to share his ideas, knowing that he will be listened to and his ideas will be valued.

Summary

The teacher input and instruction-giving part of the lesson is an exercise in communication. The need to communicate clearly to a diverse group, providing an explanation of often-new material and the actions required in response to it, is complex and we need to think carefully about *what* we are communicating and *how* we are communicating it.

Identified issue	Suggestion/Check	My action	Any impact?
How to ensure that the message you communicate is understood	It's not what you say, it's the way that you say it.		
	Are the instructions useful? Effective? Clear? How do you know?		
How to utilise questions effectively and avoid confusion	Adult use of questioning to prompt learning and promote child engagement		
	Child use of questioning to indicate learning		
	Adult response to child's questions encourage independence and confidence		
How to encourage participation in learning	Positive reinforcement		
	Physical accessibility		
	Scaffolded		
	Matching work to ability		

3 Phase 3 of the lesson: Individuals working as a class

'One of the most common challenges put to me, from parents to headteachers, both in the UK and internationally, is: "Inclusive classrooms are of course ideal, but in reality how are you supposed to meet the needs of so many different types of children? Don't they all end up losing out?" This is a perfectly reasonable and understandable question. The assumption that a teacher has to create separate curricula for multiple needs and approaches in the classroom is a myth. It is also utterly impractical.' Daniel Sobel

Once we settle a group of children to work, in an ideal world they would focus quickly and work more or less independently on the same task. Consider the scenario on the following page.

Geoffrey Leopold de Ville had been teaching Latin to teenagers for 27 years. In his favourite tweed jacket, which he bought while reading classics at Oxford, he would pace the classroom and regale the enthralled students with stories of ancient times, throwing out questions while he looked out of the window over the lacrosse and rugby pitches. Each November, as the leaves began to fall from the oak tree by the planetarium, he recited his favourite passage from Pliny the Elder and would ask the class to pen an essay about it in silence, to be handed in by the end of the lesson. As the students settled down thoughtfully and attentively to the task, he would sit at his old wooden desk at the front reading his favourite passage from The Iliad. At the end of the lesson he barely looked up as they filed past him, placing their neatly written essays on his desk.

This isn't how the average teacher in the UK experiences their average lesson. From a whole-class management perspective, there is a difference between getting individual children to learn on their own versus working in teams, groups or as a whole class. To get groups of individuals with a broad range of needs and abilities all to be working happily in silence is a fantasy – and not necessarily a good one. In an inclusive, mixed-ability classroom, it simply has no bearing on reality. But we suppose it is important to emphasise this to the teachers who think it should be and challenge their frustrations, which are born out of the fact that 'these kids just won't do as they are told'. This unrealistic expectation can be the beginning of the end for a teacher, who will soon become disillusioned, and then either turn curmudgeonly or leave the profession, or both.

How to meet a range of children's needs without endless worksheets

Getting a whole class to settle into learning independently is a real skill that requires detailed planning and practice. Arguably, this is the hardest of all classroom management tasks because you are splitting one task into at least 30, policing it and then ensuring that it's actually effective.

Sounds like an unclimbable mountain. It's not. That's not to say it's simple, but careful preparation and sound delivery will create the right conditions.

The obvious need here is to differentiate. Easy to say but to do it consistently all day every day is not something that teachers have been trained to do. It is a skill that needs honing and working out, and this chapter encapsulates the best of our thinking about how you can do it well and save yourself a lot of time and stress.

What differentiation isn't

Rightly, there is a great drive in schools to ensure that all children are treated equally, but the drive for equality often misses the fact that we do not all start in the same place. The view that 'giving extra support to certain children to meet their needs is unfair to the others' is misguided. It neglects the fact that children are not all the same. For *all* children to learn effectively we need to even the playing field so that they can *all* succeed, rather than aiming for varying, adjusted levels of success or achievement. Presenting all children with the same information and tasks in a mixed-ability class will lead to pedagogic failure and, contrary to those who harbour Victorian ideals of classrooms, it will be the teacher, not the child, who is at fault.

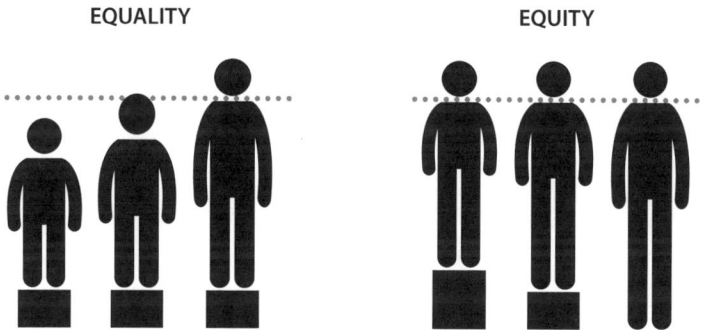

Understanding and embedding the difference between equality and equity is the root and basis of differentiation. There is a current move to talk about 'adapting', rather than 'differentiation', as has been the way in the United States. This also appears to be the newly adopted language of Ofsted (2019). This is in part because the word 'differentiation' has been given new meanings and implications in schools to imply endless worksheets and SLT demands. We would contend that this approach is a quick route to work overload and stress, and also an ineffective way of teaching. Differentiation for the majority of children is about small tweaks, quick interventions and small pieces of planned support.

What differentiation is

Differentiation follows the themes and topics of the mainstream curriculum but employs a range of approaches and resources that enable and support all children to access the learning more easily. This might make the learning more challenging for more able pupils or provide more or different support for others. We need to add one extra important element here, in line with our previous thoughts. Whatever you end up doing to fit in with this definition should not become 'repetitive' or 'box ticking' or the preparing of endless worksheets. The don'ts of differentiation are so emphatic that they almost become the essentials of the dos definition. So, let's be clear, differentiation is ineffective when it is:

- unmanageable and overburdens already overly committed and dedicated teachers, because this is both unfair and unsustainable
- about predictable, off-the-shelf differentiated worksheets, not least because this is the path to boredom

- about an entirely parallel curriculum – if anything, this unnecessary effort can further fracture superficial divides between children
- about the 'one size fits all' approach of our classics teacher.

Effective differentiation needs to be built on a culture of inclusion as we discussed on page 23. Underlying the effective differentiation needs to be a belief in inclusion and an understanding of the need to make adjustments to enable all children to be included within the school and so promote their learning. Even within this culture there are different models of differentiation and different areas that can be differentiated.

Models of differentiation

A pertinent question that has to be faced is to what extent should or can a child with significant SEND engage in the same curriculum as their peers? Though this question is more technical than pivotal – which unfortunately isn't always the case for some education writers – let's consider the three possibilities:

- differentiation within the curriculum
- a partially differentiated curriculum
- a fully differentiated curriculum.

Differentiation within the curriculum

The majority of children can be supported by 'differentiation within the curriculum' – that is with small adaptations and tweaks to support the child's access to learning at the curriculum level of the majority of their class group. These adaptations and tweaks are easy to put in place and reduce stress for the child and the teacher. They ensure that the child is fully included within the class, both socially and academically.

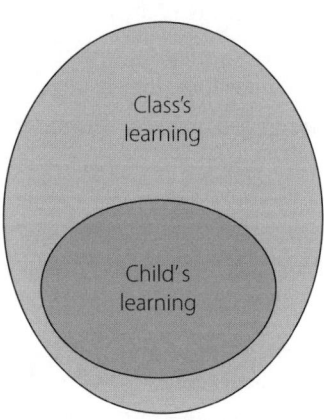

Children supported by differentiation within the curriculum are able to access the full classroom curriculum with minimal additional support, resources or time. This model of differentiation is part of high-quality teaching. It is part of what good teachers offer to all their pupils. They (and, on occasions, their TAs) use a range of strategies to support the children's learning and independence. These small tweaks make a huge difference to learning, engagement and behaviour.

Case study: Fatima

Fatima is a bright girl who is keen to do well and tries hard; however, she struggles with focus and attention. She is constantly moving and fidgeting, and regularly calls out as she struggles to regulate her enthusiasm to join in. She is able to engage in learning at the same academic level as her classmates, even though she needs differentiation to support her with focus and attention. She has an adult sitting near her during whole-class inputs so that she can whisper her answers to the teacher's questions, rather than shout them out. She also benefits from regular movement and fiddle-time breaks to help her to concentrate. With this support, she often succeeds at a higher level than many of her classmates.

Instead of this...	... try this
You have four ability groups within your class and for maths they each have a different version of the same worksheet, adapted to their level.	All the children start with the same basic task. However, some of them are working with larger or more numbers to complete it. Some use formal methods to tackle the task; some work independently; some work following modelled examples. Another group uses number lines and concrete resources. There may be a few outliers who need more differentiation using the models on the following pages.

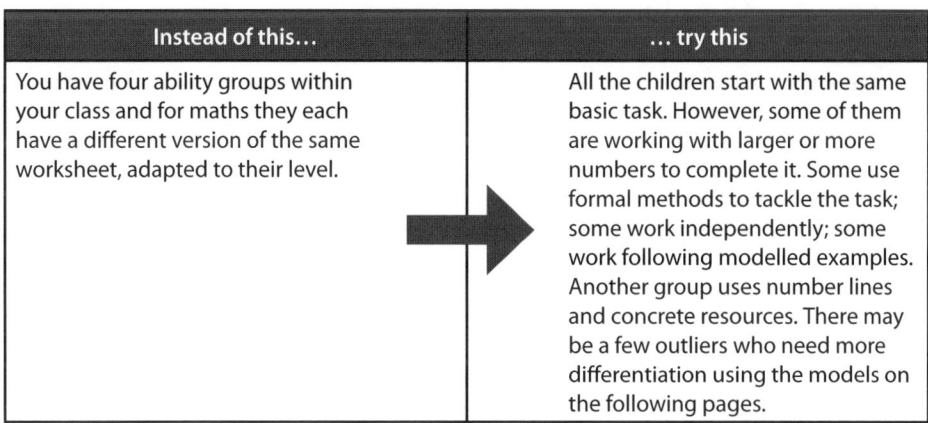

A partially differentiated curriculum

In many classes, there will be more able children or those with special needs who require significant differentiation to access or extend the main class teaching. They can access the same texts or subject areas as their peers but do so at a different level to the majority of the class.

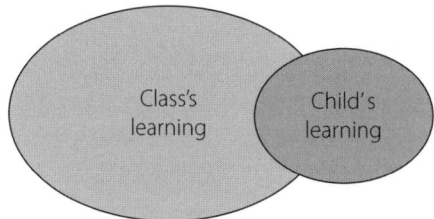

For example: the majority of the class is learning about rounding numbers to the nearest 100 using three-digit numbers, while a child (or group of children) who is working with a partially differentiated curriculum will work on rounding two-digit numbers to the nearest ten. They continue to follow the themes of the curriculum, but at a different academic level. A child may need this level of support or adjustment in one or more areas of the curriculum but be able to access learning at the same level as their peers in another.

Case study: David

David struggles with processing, particularly in maths. He works hard to recall numbers, but for him they are slippery and quickly disappear. He struggles to recall number facts. He needs regular repetition of strategies for formal methods of calculation. However, a differentiated curriculum helps him to access much of the learning. He starts each lesson with a five-minute pre-learning session to remind him of what he covered in the previous lesson and introduce any specific vocabulary he will need to use in that day's lesson. He then takes part in the whole-class input, with a TA to support him to use visual prompts to recall the vocabulary. He uses practical apparatus (such as cubes, number lines and base ten materials) to work through examples, as physically moving things helps him to recall facts and processes. When it comes to individual activities, David works in a small group with adult support. Modelled examples show him how to lay out his work, and he works through questions using concrete resources, smaller numbers and simpler vocabulary than the majority of his class. In the afternoon, David has an over-learning session, which reviews what he has learned earlier in the day, to check what he remembers and tackle any misconceptions. With this differentiated curriculum, David is able to make progress and develop his independent learning skills at his own level.

Instead of this…	… try this
You are teaching the lower-ability group, so you assume that all the children are working at the same level, and so provide them with the same work. Most of them do very little, and one boy called Oscar kicks off and storms out of the lesson.	You start your lesson with a pre-learning session to ensure that the majority of the class is confident with the vocabulary they will need for the lesson. Oscar has been given personalised visual images for two key words. He is pre-warned of the question you are going to ask him during the input and given a visual prompt to help him focus on the information for which he should listen. An adult sits near him to point to the visual prompts and help his focus.

During the individual activities, the TA goes through a differentiated activity with Oscar and sets up his task-management board, so that he can use it to help him to track his progress through the task. The TA then works with other children, regularly coming back to check in with Oscar to make sure that he is on-task and knows what to do. Oscar works carefully and quietly and completes the task. At the end of the lesson, Oscar is able to share something he has learned and done well. |

A fully differentiated curriculum

There will be a few children within many mainstream classrooms, the vast majority of whom will hopefully have an EHCP, who require a fully differentiated curriculum. They will work on the same subject areas, but at a completely different level and with different resources.

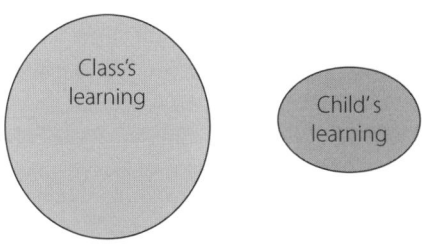

Class's learning

Child's learning

For example, while the class are working on formal addition of three-digit numbers, the child will be working on adding number bonds to ten using cubes. In most cases, the teacher and SENCO will identify when this approach is needed and then plan for the fully differentiated curriculum, to be supported by a TA. Some of these children may access part of their learning outside the classroom in focused groups to support their learning or SEMH needs. Children may need a fully differentiated curriculum in one area of learning but be able to access the mainstream learning in another.

Case study: Olena

Olena has an EHCP for additional learning needs. Despite very high levels of support, by Year 4 she is still unable to recall any phonics and struggles to write more than a few words with accuracy. She often confuses the order of the letters in her own name. However, she has lots of exciting and original ideas that she is keen to share. Though she cannot read age-appropriate texts independently, her comprehension of texts that are read to her is good. The growing gap between Olena and her peers means that she needs a fully differentiated curriculum. Olena needs additional specialist support to try to develop her literacy skills using whole-word approaches, supported by lots of visual prompts to aid her memory.

During English lessons, Olena participates fully in the speaking and listening sections. Her TA reads her the class texts. Olena then uses voice-activated software to record her ideas. Though there are clear links to what the rest of the class are doing, Olena follows a fully differentiated curriculum designed for her by the teacher and SENCO, which her TA supports her to follow. This allows her to access learning and make progress at her own level.

While accepting the reality and pressures of mixed-ability mainstream classrooms, it is our contention that the vast majority of children can and should be taught within a mainstream classroom. There are those who will need additional adult support or different or further resources, but as far as possible this support should be provided within the classroom. By developing a culture of inclusion that focuses on how children are made to feel and supported to engage by small tweaks, they can be successful within the classroom, rather than being withdrawn for endless interventions. The latter reduces their sense of belonging, further reduces their engagement and often means they do not access the quality-first teaching that is their entitlement.

What can we differentiate?

We've established that the inclusive classroom is about a cultural adaptation involving the eight Rs discussed on page 23 and that there is a technical discussion to be had around how the materials of the lesson are situated alongside or within the curriculum. There is also a more nuanced adaptation of curriculum materials that we now must consider. There are four key elements that can be tweaked to help to level children's experience of the curriculum. Let's keep in mind what we said earlier – differentiation can only really work if it doesn't take a long time to do. So, this isn't meant to be about adding more work for teachers, but about creating an instant 'go-to' model comprising four easy elements that the teacher can adapt quickly.

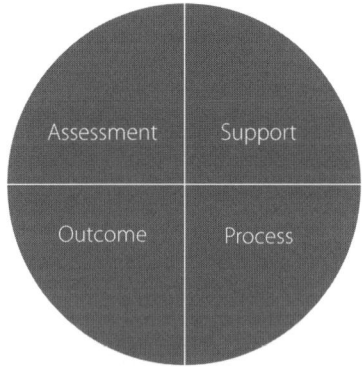

Differentiation by support

Children will need different amounts of support from an adult to access learning. But 'differentiation by support' does not mean that a child needs an adult with them at all times. Appropriate levels of support will vary and might include:

- support for part of the lesson
- a quick additional explanation
- working in a group with an adult to go through extra examples
- working one-to-one with an adult for some or part of the time
- support for engaging in different activities and tasks.

Often an adult will be able to provide a child with support for starting an activity, then leave them to work independently for a time and then return to refocus them or provide additional support. This process can be repeated throughout the lesson. There is rarely a need for an adult to be 'glued' to a child's side for a whole lesson.

Differentiation by process

These are the small tweaks we mention throughout the book that enable children to approach activities in different ways, such as using additional apparatus or visuals. This might include:

- supporting them to read written texts during the lesson
- asking different and directed questions or asking questions in different ways
- simplifying vocabulary
- using apparatus to support their understanding.

Differentiation by outcome

We can get very fixed ideas about how children should demonstrate what they have learned. Much of this is based on a traditional view that writing equals learning. At some level, we all know that writing is not always the best way to demonstrate understanding or learning, yet we can struggle to translate this into our classrooms. Much of differentiation is planning for and accepting different ways for children to share their learning, so that their writing skills do not become a barrier to their expression and sharing of learning in other areas of the curriculum.

Unfortunately, using IT is not a magic wand!

When children undergo an assessment and receive a diagnosis of some form of learning difficulty, the diagnosing practitioner will often suggest that the child uses IT, usually a laptop, to record their learning. Often parents (and teachers) will seize on this as the magic answer to the child's difficulties. IT is immensely helpful, but it takes time to develop the necessary associated skill set. To use IT effectively, children need to be able to plan what they want to write, remember what they want to write and then find the letters on the keyboard while managing the challenges of spelling and grammar. While a child is learning the skills to use IT, it can add a level of cognitive challenge that makes things more difficult rather than easier.

To use IT effectively, a child needs to be able to:

- link upper- and lower-case letters
- find letters on the keyboard
- manipulate their fingers to land on the correct keys
- understand how to save, file and find their work effectively.

These skills require a high level of cognitive demand and dexterity, and for some, this is unrealistic. For all, it is unrealistic without practice and support.

Voice-activated software can help with this, but there are difficulties where the child's speech is not clear or the software picks up background noises. The latter is always an issue in a busy classroom.

Differentiation by assessment

Increasingly, there is flexibility within the national assessment systems. Children are able to have extra time or learning breaks, work in quiet spaces and use IT within the exam system. For this to be effective, it needs to be part of the classroom practice. It is no good giving a child 25 per cent additional time in an exam if they have had to complete their practice papers in the same time as their classmates. They won't know how to use the additional time. Equally, using a computer in an exam is a very different skill to using one to record ideas in class or write an essay. These things need to be taught and practised. Yet often we don't reflect this flexibility within classroom practice, which undermines both the child's ability to use these adaptations effectively in exams and our ability to use formal assessment to support our teaching. This returns to the confusion between equality and equity we discussed at the beginning of the chapter.

But differentiation by assessment goes beyond formal assessment: it is about recognising that children show their learning in different ways and valuing this. This can include:

- oral responses
- making a model
- drama.

Differentiation by outcome is much more than an easy fix, but it can be used to help a child to demonstrate their learning in ways other than just the traditional method: writing.

Focusing on the learning

Once we know what we are planning for the children to learn and have identified how we can support them to access it, we need to consider how we enable them to focus on the point of the learning, rather than being sidetracked by the peripheries of the task. As teachers we can get very involved in the issues of presentation and the administration of the lesson, which often obscures the point of the learning.

Joel struggles in many areas, particularly his focus and his learning. His teacher is constantly irritated by how little work he does in any lesson. She complains regularly that Joel can never get started, which of course prevents him from ever finishing. It was only when she observed him being taught by another teacher that she understood the problem. Joel had to find his book and often would lose focus during this and end up with the wrong book. When he had his book, he had to find the right page and then a pencil. Again, a challenge. When he had finally achieved this, he had to copy down the date – a painstaking process, which required him to look from book to board for every letter and number. Then he needed to repeat this with the title. By this time, not only had Joel forgotten what he was supposed to be doing, but others were beginning to finish the task, adding to his sense of both panic and failure. No wonder he achieved so little. The need was to change the pattern, so he could focus on the learning and not the related administrative tasks.

Top tips for helping children to focus on the learning

As shown by Joel's case study, there is much that is expected within the classroom that relates to the learning, but it is not actual learning. While learning to manage the admin and organisation underlying any task or role is important, it is key to ensure the administrative demands do not obscure or overwhelm the learning.

Tip 1: Check that children expend their energy on the point of the learning

So often when we ask children to work on their own, we expect them to complete a number of tasks before they can start learning. These are things about which most people would be blissfully unaware. They constitute unnoticed routines or practices that we as adults understand as required through years of practice and experience: writing the date and the title, copying out learning intentions, drawing a margin. But these often become barriers and actually stop children from accessing the learning.

For many children, copying from a board or book is extremely difficult. Unless this is the focus of the activity, for example in some handwriting activities, we need to avoid this for many children. Some children will struggle to remember what they need to write, so they need to look at the board frequently, sometimes for every letter when copying a word. The process becomes difficult, slow and laborious. As a result, they frequently lose their place and it takes time and effort to find it each time they look up at the board or down at their sheet. This can be an issue even with copying something short like the date. If you are unsure how this feels, try copying out something in an unknown script. Then place the text at a distance and try it again. This is what copying from the board is like for many children with SEN.

We should not assume that because most children can copy, all children can. Many children can quickly become overwhelmed by the task of copying, so that what they are writing lacks any meaning for them. The focus of the task becomes the completing of the copying, rather than any learning from or connected with it. This means that they will struggle to complete the task, let alone access any learning related to the copied text. They will often opt out or disrupt to avoid completion of this task. Support in this area will often not only support learning, but also support behaviour. There are children who prefer to kick off and disrupt rather than copy something that they find difficult and see as pointless.

If we want children to engage in learning and be successful, we need to ensure that they are able to focus their time and energy on things that are central to the learning.

Archie was a boy in my English group with significant literacy difficulties. Over the autumn term, I got him to engage with writing. We used a range of word banks with visuals, scribing and voice-activated software to support him, so that he could record ideas and then edit them. He was beginning to engage and was feeling more positive about using writing to record his ideas. Yet during every history and geography lesson, Archie kicked off as soon as the children were asked to write. I checked – and yes, he could access scribing and the voice-activated software, so the teacher couldn't identify the problem. I talked to Archie, who would only tell me it was unfair, and he hated the teacher. So, I went to observe the lesson, and all became clear. Though he had someone to scribe and he knew that he could access IT resources, while this was being set up the teacher would tell Archie 'just' to write the date and learning intention into his book. For Archie this was a virtually impossible task, requiring all the skills he found most difficult – remembering what to write, finding information on a crowded board, copying – so rather than attempt it, he disrupted the lesson. We discussed the matter and the teacher started to give this information to Archie (and several others with literacy difficulties) printed out and ready. He stuck it into his book and began to engage in the learning.

Sara

Instead of this...	... try this
You ask all the children to copy administrative information (such as the date and title) off the board.	You provide all the children with a slip to stick into their book with this information on it, so that they can quickly focus on the learning activities, rather than the administrative tasks. Consider starting a whole-school discussion about how much of this information is really needed and cutting it to a minimum.

Tip 2: Think about how the children can show their learning

We need to think not only about what the learning *is*, but how we ask children to *demonstrate* it. There is an underlying belief among some teachers, TAs and even children that it is not 'proper' learning unless it is demonstrated in handwritten work. This belief makes life more difficult for many children and is pretty outdated. Think about how little actual handwriting you do in your daily life. The chances are that the majority of your writing is on some form of electronic device. An insistence on handwriting is not realistic preparation for adult life. Unfortunately for many children, it continues to be realistic preparation for the exam system.

Case study: Albie

Albie loves history. He is fascinated by the interactions of historical figures. He can not only recall a myriad of facts about key figures from the Tudor period, but he can also use this information to discuss and explain the events of the period with exceptional understanding and maturity. On the basis of this, he is an outstanding history student. However, Albie struggles to record more than a simple sentence without support. To ask Albie to show his learning in writing not only undermines his enthusiasm and skills as a historian but also devalues his learning. We need to be more imaginative in how we ask him to show his learning. What could work better for him?

This is reinforced by many senior leaders, who want written evidence of verbal feedback and practical work. We know one school where after a drama lesson, every child must stick into their book a note explaining that they did drama and describing what they learned, adding in a handwritten statement giving their view. This doesn't extend or embed the learning but simply provides written evidence that the lesson happened and proves that the class did something. We cannot help but feel that this laborious process is rather fruitless and will only ensure that the children place value only on learning or experiences about which they have to write something.

Often children are asked to copy something that an adult has written, so that it is in their handwriting. Typically, a child with literacy difficulties dictates to an adult, who records their ideas. The child then is expected to copy down what the adult has written. The question is, 'Why?'. The child has shared their ideas and recorded their learning. Copying what an adult has written seems to us to be a waste of time, if they can share their learning verbally. The message that is being given is that dictating their ideas is not a proper way of recording learning and that it is only *real* learning if *they* write it. If we are providing alternative ways of recording learning, we need to show that these are respected and valued, and not just for those who can't physically write.

There is a further issue for senior leaders here. We have worked with a number of secondary schools where a significant number of SEN children have adults scribing for them in some or all lessons. If a child has been disempowered from recording themselves, having had access to an adult scribe in certain lessons, what do they do in lessons when this isn't offered, and how can they be prepared for adult life? In many of these schools, we also found that at least half of the children had happily and effectively used IT to record their learning at their primary schools. The curriculum leads in the secondary schools claimed that the children didn't want to use IT because it added to their sense of being 'different'. But was this assertion just an excuse for avoiding buying laptops or dealing with the difficulties in moving them around a school building?

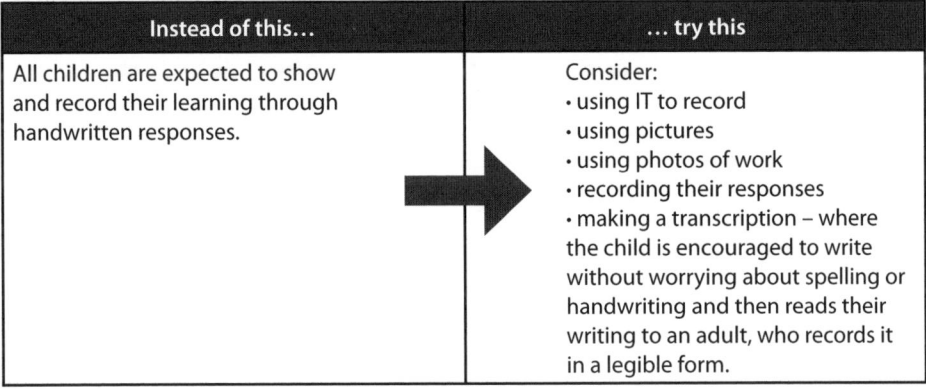

Instead of this...	... try this
All children are expected to show and record their learning through handwritten responses.	Consider: • using IT to record • using pictures • using photos of work • recording their responses • making a transcription – where the child is encouraged to write without worrying about spelling or handwriting and then reads their writing to an adult, who records it in a legible form.

With a little imagination, we can think of a wide range of ways in which children can display their learning. It is important that we both utilise and value these responses. Different children can be asked to record their learning in different ways.

Making writing easier

There are many ways to make recording and writing easier. The Communication Trust's No Pens Day is part of a wider initiative to consider different ways of recording learning. Equally there are many ways to make writing easier for children and more effective for recording learning.

Tip 1: Making note-taking easier for those with difficulties recording

Note-taking is a skill. Many teachers find this relatively easy and so forget that it might be difficult for some or all of the children they teach – though it is interesting how few teachers are keen to take minutes at a meeting! Also, there is an assumption in schools that *someone* should teach this core skill, but many English teachers feel that they would struggle to see how they'd have time for this in an already packed curriculum. However, note-taking needs to be taught and modelled, and children shown that it is different in different contexts. This includes, for instance, the use of abbreviations and symbols that make sense and that the note-taker will understand later.

> *As a student many years ago, when I came to revise from my geography notes, I discovered that I had used 'dev' to stand for development, developed, developing, device, Devon and various other random words that may or may not have begun with 'dev'. Of course, this made my notes virtually impossible to understand. Such behaviour is not restricted to children with dyslexia.*
>
> *Sara*

Instead of this...	... try this
You ask all the children to take notes as you explain the story of the War of the Roses, without providing them with any framework or structure for their note-taking.	Give the children a copy of the slides from which you are teaching and let them annotate them. Remember that this annotation will also need to be taught as a skill. It is good preparation for further study, and this is a standard support for students with dyslexia in many universities.
	Alternatively, provide a scaffold that the child can slot information into as you speak, rather than making notes from scratch on a blank piece of paper. A colleague of Sara's used to get children to design these as part of their revision, so the children could pick out key themes and points.

Tip 2: Fear of starting

For many of us when writing, it is not the process and physical action of writing that is difficult, but the difficulties of starting. Ask any writer how many times they have tidied their sock drawer rather than actually put pen to paper or finger to keyboard, even when they know what they want to say. How much more difficult is it for *children* when they are not sure what they want to say?

This can be made easier in several ways:

- Use of IT: So many of us use IT to record and it is the default preference of many children and a good preparation for adulthood. It needs to be remembered that if children are going to use IT effectively, they need to be trained to name their work and save it somewhere that they can find it again.

- Use of individual whiteboards to record: Writing on a board removes the fear of a permanent first mark, and so enables children to take risks. Try to avoid children having to copy what they have written on a board into their books.

- Reconstructing sentences: If you have a child working at sentence level, rather than writing a dictated sentence out for the child to copy, write the sentence onto a strip of paper. Reread it with the child. Then cut the sentence up, so that each word is separate. Muddle the pieces up and get the child to reconstruct the sentence in the correct order, and then stick the pieces into their book.

- Completing sentence stems: Write a sentence stem for a child to complete, such as *'After lunch, we…'*. The use of sentence stems or scripts enables children to use a series of set phrases, such as *'I think… because…'*, to introduce their ideas and get them started on their recording. It reduces the fear of the blank piece of paper. These are also useful to use in oral work when children are struggling to express their ideas in a sentence.

- Adapting model sentences: Write a model sentence for the child to use, changing the key words or ideas: *'The girl jumped out of the window and ran away'* could become, through questioning and prompting (such as 'Which girl?' and 'How did she run?'), *'The princess leaped out of the window and sprinted away.'*

Tip 3: Knowing when the task is complete

For many children, not understanding when they have finished a task or what the completed task looks like can act as a barrier to starting the task. Think about how nervous you would be if asked to start on a journey to a new destination without any guidance about the route. Yet this is in effect what we ask children to do on a daily basis. Key to supporting a child to start more confidently is being clear about the expected outcome and what they are expected to do to achieve it. This can be done by modelling and showing examples of a completed task.

Instead of this...		... try this
You announce the task and say that it should be completed in 20 minutes.	→	You show the children an example completed by a child in a previous year, so that they understand the expectation. Also, ensure that they understand the steps to get there.

Other ideas to try

Here are a couple of additional tips to support writing and make it easier for children to engage with it:

- Use a checklist to show what the child needs to do or include. This can act as a reminder and a measure of progress through the task.

- For closed tasks like a maths calculation, use clear and visual measures of success. For example, put out a set of cubes, one for each calculation, and two pots. Each time the child completes a calculation, they move a cube from the first pot to the second pot. When all the cubes are moved, the task is finished. It is important to recognise that the task is completed and not be tempted to add further elements.

How to support individuals working alongside each other

For many children with SEN, there are issues related not only to their learning, but also to the impact of their needs on others in their class. We have had to deal over the years with a number of complaints from parents who were upset that children with SEN were disrupting their children's education in some way. We need to ensure that *all* the children in the classroom are able to enjoy an environment that is supportive of their learning and of their individuality. The benefits to 'neurotypical' children from sharing their classroom with a child with SEN are far greater than any negative impact on their learning: being able to work with a range of people is a core life skill; appreciating that everyone is different makes for happier children; and appreciating that we can learn not just from the teacher but through our interactions is key to successful socialisation. It's clear to us that SEN should not detract in any way from anyone. It should not be an 'either–or' choice of 'educate my child or their child properly but you can't do both at the same time'. This position is founded on a lack of understanding of what is possible, let alone what is best for either child.

Managing distraction

One of the issues with many of the supports we put in place for children is that they are by their nature distracting for other learners. Equally, the other children can act as a distraction for the child using the support strategies. Many children will distract, disrupt and interrupt when they:

- are uncertain
- want to avoid a task
- think that they cannot achieve or succeed.

It is vital that we try to understand what the children and their behaviour are trying to communicate and that we respond to that, not just the behaviour, however disruptive it is. Think about the class clown and the different things they might be trying to communicate. Too often we respond to the behaviour, not the communication. By doing this we can make matters worse, as we are providing neither the support nor the help the child may crave. This means that they are still unable or unwilling to attempt the task and now are feeling resentful and upset because we didn't respond as they wanted.

Effective behaviour management, or, to put it better, responding effectively to children's communication through behaviour, is a topic for a whole new book. But, in our experience, the strategies we share in this book can have an astounding impact on behaviour.

Working in silence versus self-talk

At the beginning of this chapter, we looked at Geoffrey Leopold de Ville's imaginary class. He expected his class to work in silence. However, by doing so we can deprive children of the opportunity to work with others to support their learning or using self-talk to support themselves. However much we try to deny it – and society tells us that those who talk to themselves are 'mad' – we all use self-talk to help us remember what we are doing and to complete tasks. For children, this is often a skill that needs to be taught: both how to make self-talk useful and that it is an acceptable strategy for learning. This requires adults to model self-talking and verbalise their thinking as they complete a task. For example: 'To cut this carrot, I must hold it still while making sure that my fingers are clear of the knife, so that I don't cut myself. I need to use a chopping board, so I don't damage the table.' This needs to be combined with modelling the task, so that the child can see how to hold the knife and the carrot.

Self-talk is also important for developing and promoting self-esteem. Think how often we tell ourselves that we 'can do it' to encourage ourselves.

In a low-attaining literacy group, one of the major barriers to the children's progress was identified as their poor self-image as learners and writers.

To tackle this, their teacher identified and verbalised the children's beliefs about themselves, which she described as the 'gremlins' that stopped them writing. The teacher considered the positive actions that they could take to overcome these gremlins. Then she started the lessons with a bit of 'gremlin-bashing'. The children hit the imaginary 'gremlins' with imaginary mallets. It rather baffled the visiting inspector, who asked a child what they were doing. Seb then explained he was 'beating gremlins' and showed the inspector what he could do, now that he had squashed his gremlins, who had been stopping him writing. His progress was recognised as 'outstanding'.

Furthermore, self-talk plays an important role in emotional regulation by identifying and naming feelings, so that children are more able to manage and regulate their emotions. Some of the self-talk can and should be internal, but particularly for young children and those learning to use this to manage their emotions, they need to name and express their feelings aloud.

Instead of this...	... try this
The teacher enforces strict silence in the classroom for all individual tasks.	Ask for quiet for writing tasks but ensure that those working with an adult or peer are able to continue to converse and those who need to talk to themselves can. Use a 'volume thermometer' to show the voice level expected, so it is relatively quiet for those who need this to help their focus.

Issues of working in silence

There are vast variations in schools' expectations of acceptable working noise, from 'a working buzz' to 'everyone works in silence'. There are arguments in favour of both extremes but, as always, the best view is to fit the noise level to the learning that is expected. However, in terms of working with challenging and vulnerable pupils, there are a number of issues to consider.

Pros of working in silence	Cons of working in silence
• Quiet can be calming for children with sensory needs. • For children with sensory issues, noise can be more than just a distraction. It can add to and induce sensory overload. • For many children, quiet can support concentration and focus. • It is good practice for exams.	• For many children, trying to stay silent is very difficult. If you say that absolute silence must be maintained, you are putting yourself in a position where you are telling children off for things they cannot help, such as verbal twitches and body noises. • By demanding silence, you are setting a standard that is hard to maintain, which means that you are likely to clash with children, and it will be easy for them to 'wind you up' if they wish. Frequently, the learning can be lost to disputes about noise level. • If all the class has to work in silence, it makes any child who is working with an adult stand out. This can act as a disincentive for them to engage with the adult and seek the support they need for their learning. • Working in silence inhibits self-talk to support learning.

Remember that headphones work well for those who want or need a quieter classroom and are an essential for anyone using voice-activated software or software that reads back what the child has written.

Summary

Differentiation has become misunderstood in teaching to imply extra work and stress for the teacher. We hope in this book in general, and this chapter in particular, to challenge that view. It sounds obvious to say that enabling children to focus on the key points of the learning promotes and supports their engagement and progress. But in the reality of the busy classroom, facilitating a clear and simple focus in the midst of a lesson that pulls the teacher in lots of directions is where the real value of a simple approach to differentiation based on small tweaks and adaptations comes into its own. See the summary checklist on page 106.

Identified issue	Suggestion/Check	My action	Any impact?
How to meet a range of children's needs without endless worksheets	How bespoke or personalised is the differentiation for individuals?		
	How much time does the differentiation take to prepare? Does it feel manageable?		
What can we differentiate?	Differentiation by support		
	Differentiation by process		
	Differentiation by outcome		
	Differentiation by assessment		
Focusing on the learning	Does the differentiation support independence and engagement?		
	How does the differentiation support children to record their learning in a range of ways?		
	How does the differentiation support language acquisition, cognitive stretching, comprehension and articulation?		

4 Phase 4 of the lesson: Inclusive group work

Chapter overview

'The greatest benefits and challenges for children working in the classroom can both be delivered through group work. It takes careful management, planning and the explicit teaching of group work skills to ensure the benefits outweigh the challenges.' Sara Alston

Picture the scene:

A group of eight children is asked to plan a drama presentation. Lana suggests an idea that she thinks is sensible and interesting, but one of the other students interjects, 'No, that's not going to work.' The group continues to explore other suggestions, but Lana is stuck thinking about what appeared to her as a rejection. She feels deeply that she has been publicly embarrassed and admonished despite other students in her group also having their ideas dismissed. She sits looking into the distance as the group continues to work together, with her mind navigating various catastrophising thoughts about how everyone thinks she is stupid and hates her. After 15 minutes, she cannot take it any longer and runs to the toilets and cries.

Reece, also part of the group, sits in the circle but isn't really following the conversation. He doesn't understand what everyone is talking about because he hadn't been able to follow the instructions or remember any of the topic materials they had covered so far. He effects his 'smile and nod' and then, after a bit, brings out his 'messing around tactics' of throwing little bits of paper at another student, which he knows will spark a tussle and a laugh.

Examples like these happen all the time in the 'Wild West' of group work. No teacher (the authors included) ever want such upsets or frustrations to emerge, but they do; they are going to happen. They can also have longer and more far-reaching consequences than one might perceive in the classroom. You can imagine these students going home and feeling deeply the pain of the mini-exclusion: feeling like they don't belong or aren't good enough. This is a self-judgement based on children's perceptions of others in their group. Some of these children might remember this moment for a long time and use it as an excuse not to bother 'trying' in future group work or social interactions. We are reminded of the viciousness of the children in *Lord of the Flies*, which may be unconscious, unintentional or even non-existent but perceived. Possibly some of the worst forms of bullying and exclusion can happen within groups. Therefore, the purpose of this chapter is to:

1. help you to organise group work in a way that doesn't lead to the unintended exclusion of children
2. help you to utilise groups to their maximum potential.

Benefits and challenges of group work

At times, the challenges of managing group work successfully can seem overwhelming and we are aware that it is a 'high-stakes' activity in any classroom. We hope in this section to share some of the benefits and ways of making group work easier and less stressful for the adults and children.

Benefits of group work

We should start with the good news about groups for some encouragement and positive thinking before we get into the danger zone. What is so good about working in groups?

- Group work is an opportunity to promote and build inclusion within the classroom and teach inclusive attitudes and skills to the next generation.
- It can provide an opportunity for children to work with different people and develop an understanding of each other's and their own strengths and difficulties.
- We want children to be active in exploring and learning for themselves. Groups provide a way of doing this without the direct guidance of the teacher.

- Groups are ways for children to learn core skills, such as listening, presenting and debating.

- It's perfectly human to feel that it is easier and nicer to work with a friend or in a group. We have people to bounce ideas off and the shared momentum can enable us to achieve the unexpected. In other words, we human beings also learn socially. We could write a whole book about this, but I am sure you can easily grasp this notion. In other words, it's natural to learn and want to learn in groups.

- Many professions (and even the teaching profession sometimes!) rely on group participation, from surgeons to builders, rubbish collectors to lawyers. There's a myriad of groups and our participation is often key to career and life progression. Consequently, it can be argued that developing our ability to work with others is a core life skill and one that schools should be building in their children as much as preparing them for exams.

- The need for group work is built into the curriculum, particularly in English and PE, where it can actively support learning. It provides variety in the classroom. It is an opportunity for children to learn from each other. The majority of children enjoy it. And, let's be honest, it produces less marking.

Of course, just sitting in a classroom is being part of a group setting; playgrounds and lunchtimes are groups of sorts too. Everything about school life requires some group skills and this echoes society. For this reason, group work should not be thought of as simply another 'teaching technique' but as one of the ultimate goals of our education system.

Case study: Yusuf

Yusuf had significant communication and learning difficulties. He would avoid interaction with adults and children. Being asked the simplest questions, such as to respond to the register, would cause him visible anxiety. His greatest strength was in practical technology activities. Much of his learning was supported through individual technology projects. Knowing this, his teachers were able to build on his willingness in working with others. Although he continued to speak rarely, he was willing and able to demonstrate to other children how to complete technology tasks. As he became more confident, other children began to recognise his skills in this area and would ask for Yusuf to be in their group for technology activities. As Yusuf was able to share his area of strength with others, his teachers could use group work to develop his social skills, confidence and understanding.

In the example on page 109, Yusuf (and, indeed, those who worked with him) benefited massively from the group. Teachers do need to be mindful, however, of such group work backfiring and a child, like Yusuf, being harmed by negative interactions that aren't carefully monitored.

There's a well-read meme that says something to the effect of:

'Having a child with special needs isn't in any way a problem; it's having a child who doesn't include them that is.'

This whole book, like many others, looks at how we can best include children with learning difficulties, but actually, the biggest challenge is getting neurotypical children to include children with SEN in their social and learning groups. Arguably, the biggest benefit of group work is teaching all children to be inclusive.

'When groups are supported to work well, they can solve every one of the biggest challenges of inclusion: the foundation is "belonging".' Daniel Sobel

Challenges of group work

The positives of group work are clear, but for many children (and indeed adults), working in a group is not easy and it can induce anxiety. To operate well in a group requires skills that need explicit teaching, both academic and social. For those who do not find working with others easy, working as part of a group is often asking them to do two things that they find difficult simultaneously: engaging in academic learning and using their social skills.

Working with others can make children's difficulties more visible both to themselves and to others. The word might be 'exposing'. When working on their own, those who struggle to read or write can mask this from the majority of the class. When forced to work in a group, their difficulties are brought to the fore and put on show for others to see. It can be fascinating during a CPD session, when teachers are asked to record ideas on a flip chart, how many start to make excuses about their spelling and handwriting. Immediately they become nervous and aware of the real or imaginary weaknesses in their core skills. Think how much more pronounced this must be for children.

In response to their inhibitions, you may act firm to ensure that they engage but this can easily be perceived by the child as being quite brutal, and pushing on any vulnerability can lead to a child closing down. So, to make group work successful and safe for children, we need to put protective practices around them. Let's look at some more of the pitfalls and dangers of group working that can lead to this kind of negative experience.

'For many, the stress of working with others, managing social situations and the requisite demands involved can add a whole new set of difficulties that impact their ability to access the task at hand, yet group work is something we do in the classroom all the time.'
Daniel Sobel

Ghettoising reinforces stereotypes and the status of children when the less able are always put with the less able and the more able are put with the more able. It is all too easy to put children into groups on the basis of where they sit in the class, so they work in groups with those sitting in their immediate vicinity. However, it is likely that your seating plan is based on ability and/or friendships. But that does not mean that these combinations of children are the most appropriate for group work.

Case study: Year 6 class learning about Nelson Mandela

A class of Year 6 pupils was asked to produce a PowerPoint presentation to explain who Nelson Mandela was and why he should be remembered. For this task they were put in groups according to their literacy table places. When the children came to share their learning, the group of those achieving above-age expectations in English had produced a series of slides that include a detailed and clear explanation of Mandela's role and legacy, while those who were not meeting age-related literacy expectations produced a more technically proficient and interesting PowerPoint, but included little information about Mandela himself. The question is: was the key learning to produce a technically interesting PowerPoint presentation, or to learn about Mandela, or to work in a group? In this case both groups consolidated their core learning strengths, but neither learned much that was new to them.

This is an example of how a group set up to help and support each other to work together are actually hindering each other in their learning, as they are reinforcing what they already know and their core skills, rather than extending and developing them.

The key with group work is to balance academic challenges and social demands:

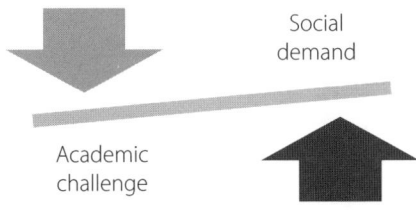

Social demand

Academic challenge

The greater the academic demands that we are making of a child, the lower we should make the social demands and vice versa.

> *I remember learning about this concept early in my career; it was a game-changer. All these years later, it remains valid. For those children who are socially confident and adept at working with others, group work can often make things easier, but this is not true for all in our classrooms.*
>
> *Sara*

The key message here is that if a piece of learning makes a high *social* demand on a child, we need to reduce the *academic* learning demand. Equally, if a piece of learning makes a high *academic* demand, we need to reduce the *social* demand and allow the child to work in the way they find socially most comfortable. In the case of groups, if we are asking a child to tackle new material or learning in an area they find particularly difficult, we should minimise the social demands by allowing them to work on their own or in a very small group. Equally, when the learning is something that they feel confident with, we can increase the social demands. Think back to the case study of Yusuf earlier in this chapter. Yusuf was able to make strides socially when he was working with practical technology tasks, as he felt confident with the academic demands and others respected his skills and understanding in this area.

If you watch very young children in the free flow of an Early Years classroom, they play and learn on their own and by working with others. As their social skills develop, they move from 'playing alongside' to working together. In this process, they find and develop groups of friends with whom they play and work well. As children mature, they become more confident to work with a greater range of people and even begin to appreciate their different skills. In most classes, there are those who are respected and valued by the other children for their expertise in certain subjects or sports. Successful group work nurtures and extends this, so all are able to develop and share their skills with others. However, we need to make it explicit what different children can bring to a group. Without this, children will focus on the obvious skills others display and will not understand or appreciate less visible or discernible skills, such as uniting a group or diffusing tensions. This requires a recognition of the useful and relevant social skills, in addition to academic prowess.

The classroom group can represent an experience of a microcosm of all groups: how you participated in your classroom when you were at school may well indicate how you feel in general about groups today. Famously, Jean-Paul Sartre wrote: 'Hell is other people'; although the philosophers among you will be able to understand the deeper meaning and context of his words, there is much of worth in the face-value meaning: that the group can be a living hell. So, what are we aiming for? Why even try?

Precisely where this danger mark lies can be found in the equally important potential benefits:

- a sense of belonging
- self-belief and worth
- peer recognition
- developing and extending social skills
- learning to engage as an equal
- a safe space to try things.

All the potential dangers can be seen here in reverse:

Group work is heaven.	Group work is hell.
I belong.	I don't belong.
I have friends.	I have no friends.
My voice is worthy.	My voice is not worthy.
I feel safe to try.	I don't feel safe to try.

Issues in social interactions

Working in a group requires social interaction, and so successful group working requires a level of social communication skills and understanding. For many children with SEN this is an area of difficulty. For these children to be successful in group working, not only do they need to be taught the skills to engage with group work, but those with whom they are working also need to be supported to develop the skills to engage with and encourage them. These are core life skills for both groups. Social interaction is a two-way process and involves not only being able to communicate but also listening to and understanding others' communications.

Social interactions involve understanding the language being used, both verbal and non-verbal. Just as children need to learn the key vocabulary to access academic learning (think back to our ideas about pre-learning in the chapter on Phase 1 of the lesson (page 60), they need to learn the verbal and non-verbal indicators that people may use in communicating with them.

Case study: Ava and Aidan

A mixed-ability group of 14-year-olds are working together on a drama project. They need to produce a short sketch on the subject of abuse. As instructed, they start by going round and each sharing an idea. Ava takes charge and points to each person in turn. When she gets to Aidan, he just shakes his head and looks at his feet. The group moves on and others share ideas. Ava starts to sum up and declares that they should focus on domestic abuse. Aidan then looks up and begins to make 'umming' noises. Ava glances his way and continues. The others begin to contribute ideas, talking over each other. Aidan continues to make quiet vocalisations that no one registers. As the others become more animated, Aidan withdraws. He has no idea how to share his real experiences of living with domestic abuse.

Aidan was not ready to share his ideas when he was first asked and is not sure how to interject later. In Ava's view, he was given his slot and didn't take it. It is now a free-for-all and if he can't push his way in, it is not her problem. The other pupils lack the skills (and possibly the interest) to understand how to support Aidan to share his thoughts.

It is only when the teacher spots what is happening and intervenes that the other pupils quieten and slowly Aidan begins to share his thoughts. The others, even Ava, begin to listen. What Aidan says changes their sketch from a pedestrian piece of work based on a soap opera plot to a moving piece of acting based on Aidan's ideas, which his group had extended.

Working in a group requires more than just an understanding of the conventions of turn-taking in conversation; it requires the skill of disagreeing politely with others. Every time Sara starts a CPD session, she reminds the participants of the need to challenge others constructively and to ensure they challenge *what* the person is saying, rather than challenging the *person*. For many children and adults, understanding that someone may hold a different view is very difficult, and it is even more difficult to accept it may have validity. Just watch any political debate or spend any time on social media to see how many adults struggle with this.

At this point the temptation is to give up on group work; it seems too complicated to be worthwhile. However, we need to remember that, as with many other learning skills, such as reading or writing, working effectively with others needs to be taught, and the requisite skills can improve and develop over time. The problem is that we assume that it is easy and an intrinsic skill that does not need to be taught. This may be where so much group work goes wrong: we don't teach how to do it and how to disagree effectively.

Case study: William

William has social communication difficulties and is very impulsive. He is always keen to work with others, but his idea of working with others is telling them what to do and then having a meltdown if they don't agree with him. It was clear that this was not sustainable in the classroom and was increasing William's social isolation. His teacher was tempted by the idea that William just worked on his own, but this would deprive him of the chance to develop the skills he would need in the future. After much thought, she and the SENCO started to develop a clear set of rules for working in groups for William, so that he had set tasks and an explicit role to follow. It was also made clear to him what other members of the group would do. These tasks were explained to him and supported by visual prompts, so he could remind himself during the activity of what he and others needed to do. He was encouraged to engage successfully in a group through the reward of time with the school's guinea pigs. It was not easy, and William continues to find working in a group very difficult, but it is slowly getting better.

Key sensory issues in group work

A further issue for many with special needs in relation to group work is the issue of sensory needs. If the norm within a classroom is to be sat at a table, with occasional excursions to sit on the carpet in the lower school years, then group work is going to create a change and sensory issue simply because people are in different places. Furthermore, when the teacher is instructing from the front, there is a single voice in the room. During individual working there might be an increase in noise level as individuals talk to their neighbour or adults. Equally there may be silence as each individual works on their own. Either way, group work entails more people speaking in the room at any one time, probably a minimum of one per group, so group work is noisier than other classroom activities.

In addition to the increased noise, group work also entails a greater level of movement in the room. Furniture may be moved. Children will move out of their set places and may move around to select and collect resources. There will be an unusual level of hustle and bustle. For many children this can be distracting and will impact on their focus and ability to concentrate; for some it can be overwhelming and, without careful management, could be a barrier to learning.

Logan was adopted from care. He struggles with sensory issues. He manages in class with support much of the time, though he struggles with change and transitions, even within the classroom. He finds group work very difficult: too much noise, too much movement and too much unpredictability, as well as the demands of working with others. Logan wants quiet and to be able to control his environment and the people within it. Staff worked hard to pre-warn Logan about group work, ensuring that he understood the task and his role in the group. But often it was still too much for him and Logan ended up having a meltdown and storming out of the room. It was clear that another approach was needed. Having talked about the problem with Logan, it was decided that Logan's group would always be placed nearest the door. Logan was given a 'secret sign' by his teacher that he could use to indicate that he was finding it overwhelming and needed to leave the room for a short time. The simple step of knowing that he could leave the room supported Logan to manage his sensory overload and slowly he became more able to manage group work. He found that wearing ear defenders also helped him.

Logan's case study demonstrates the need for us to try to pre-empt difficulties. Though avoidant behaviours can appear profound, often only simple tweaks are needed to improve a situation.

At their very worst, group activities can lead children to experience mental health issues, suicidal ideation and self-exclusion for long periods. Children often cite incidents that happened in a group scenario in a class as being the major 'cause' of their distress when, in fact, it is the tip of a bigger iceberg that involves many factors. It is just that children can see it manifested most clearly in the group setting. It may appear overly anxious to emphasise just how badly groups can go wrong but the bigger, more tragic cases are in a way obvious. It's the undercurrent of judgements and mini-exclusions that can be happening on your watch, right under your nose, that you need some skill to spot. The inherent problem is that you cannot police every group all the time and devote yourself to protecting the feelings of every child in reaction to their peers. You simply cannot judge and control all the communications and interactions. If you could, this would perhaps defeat the purpose of the group! The danger and pitfalls are very real, and they are there. So, what can you do to manage the groups in a way that doesn't quash the freedoms of exploratory social learning, while keeping all children safe and nurtured? This requires a bit of planning and thinking ahead, as outlined in the next sections.

A toolkit for inclusive group work

All too often the practicalities of group work seem overwhelming. We hope that this toolkit will help you overcome the difficulties so you can use group work to promote inclusion.

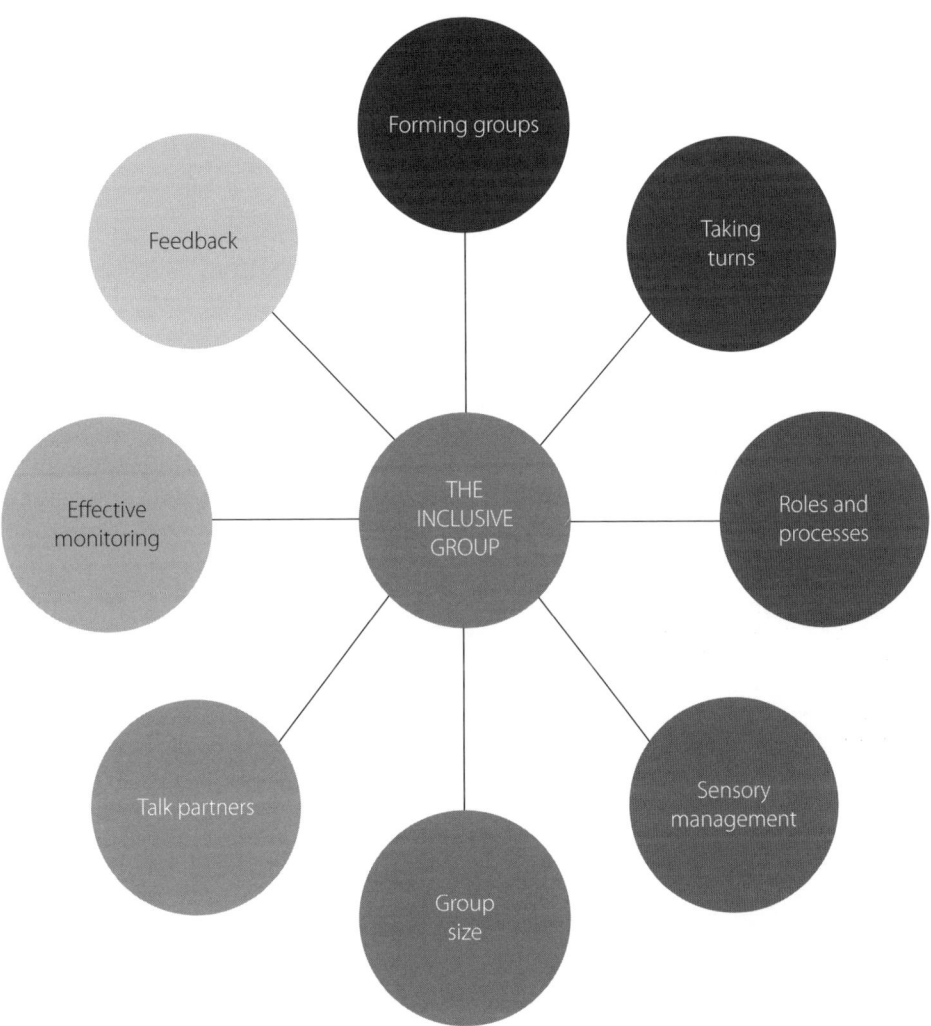

Grouping children

There are many issues to consider when putting children into groups. It is very tempting to tell the children to get into groups and leave them to get on with it but, as with any other aspect of group work, we need to think about this and plan it.

Instead of this...		...try this
You count round the room and put all the ones in a group and the twos in another and so on to create mixed-ability groups.	➡	Identify the different skills needed to undertake the learning and then match them to the strengths of the children in the class. Organise the groups so each group includes children with a mixture of skills.

Tip 1: Consider friendship groups

We all know that some children work better with those in their friendship group. It gives them confidence and security. They have some understanding of how those people think and will behave. Yet, for others, working with their friends can quickly descend into chaos with little being done. However, for children with social communication difficulties and mental health issues, the opportunity to choose at least one person they want to work with may increase their willingness and ability to engage in group work.

It is very easy to put the children with SEN together, so that on the occasions when you have an additional adult in the room, the adult can support them. However, when the adult is not there, those children can be excluded from the learning. It also discounts the significant impact of learning from peers and peer modelling. This can be a difficult balance as you want your most able children to have opportunities for stretch and challenge from their peers and not to put them in a position where they are in the role of a 'student teacher'.

It is worth periodically asking children whom *they* want to work with, ideally written down so others don't see. The answers are often surprising and illuminating.

Tip 2: Ability groups versus mixed-ability groups

This mirrors an ongoing national debate. But in the context of group work in class, it is worth considering what kind of grouping would work best for the planned task. Also consider:

- the issue of an able child who feels that they need to 'carry' less able classmates, and so become resentful of group work where they feel they are being forced into the role of teacher
- the child with learning needs who feels that their difficulties are being exposed by being put to work by those who don't share them
- the child whose difficulties often mask their talents but are able to demonstrate them to the benefit of all, by working in a group.

Tip 3: Ensure all the children understand that they are part of the group

Many children with social communication difficulties struggle to understand that when someone addresses a group, that includes them. This is why we recommend 'name tagging'. This is simply saying the children's names and ensuring that you have their attention before you speak. This not only helps the child to pay attention to your message but reinforces their inclusion in the group being addressed. For children with these difficulties, it is key to make explicit to them that they are part of the group. This often needs to be done visually. For many children, a simple list with the name of the group and names of the children in the group is sufficient.

There are children who will struggle to remember which group they are in, even when the group work is a daily occurrence. They will need the support of daily visual reminders. For example, they may need photographs of the people in the group, often within a box or circle to show that they go together. This can be done with a board with Velcro™ where the pictures and group name can be added. The physical act of seeing themselves added to a group with others can support understanding of this concept.

Supporting turn-taking

A key skill for effective group work is turn-taking. This is something that many children find difficult, particularly when they are enthusiastic about an activity and keen to share their ideas. It is a skill that takes time to develop and is a skill that, for many, needs explicit teaching. Most teachers will have come across an eight-year-old who seems to interrupt and jump in seemingly without regard for others, and secondary teachers will know of 14-year-olds who seem not to be able to control their interruptions either in class or in groups. It is likely that they haven't yet developed the quite complex brain function of 'listening and responding' or 'waiting to take my turn'. It's inappropriate to admonish a child for a physical disability and, likewise, your frustration or upset is unlikely to help them develop the skills they need but simply contribute to their already well-developed sense of 'not being good enough'. With this in mind, be careful to keep them reined in while protecting the others in the group, while at the same time not making them feel bad. We are not suggesting that this is an easy skill for any teacher – you just need to look at any debate stage or adult forum for contributing ideas to see how hard it is to facilitate. A simple idea is to acknowledge what the student has said and ask them to contribute a bit more when you call on them again because another student is just finishing their point. Don't forget – this is teaching too! You are teaching that individual but, more importantly, you are demonstrating to the other students in the class how to respond when one of their peers interrupts during group work.

Instead of this...	...try this
You put children in a group, give them the task and leave them to get on.	Prepare and discuss how to take turns and communicate what each child wants to say. This includes learning about the different ways people may communicate when they want to speak. Also, give children 'thinking time'.

Strategies to support turn-taking

Often it is easier for children to take turns if it is organised for them or there is a visual prompt to remind them who is speaking. Suggestions to support this include:

- Moving around the circle: Move around the circle so each person has a chance to speak in turn, even if they then pass. This can work at one level. However, often people want to make their contribution out of turn, and it loses its relevance if it is not a direct response to another's contribution.

- Use of a speaking object: You can only speak if you are holding the object. This can stop interruptions, but it is not always easy for a child to indicate that they want the object and are keen to speak.

- Cards: Each member of the group has a card that they turn over to indicate their desire to speak. This supports those who find it difficult to give or understand non-verbal indicators that they wish to speak. There remain issues of deciding who should speak first when a number of children are showing their cards.

There are many other non-verbal ways of indicating that someone wants to speak in a group. In school, the most traditional way is 'hands up', but this requires someone (the teacher) to choose and manage the order of the speakers. Other strategies that support this in group work include:

- Timers: When certain children tend to dominate, it can work to give each child a sand timer that they have to turn over when they are speaking. This provides an automatic time limit. They can use it all in one block or they can spread their time over a number of interventions, encouraging children to plan what they want to say more carefully before they speak. However, this can be difficult to manage as children often forget to turn over their timers. Further, it can put additional pressure on nervous speakers or those with word-finding difficulties.

- Keeping a tally of who is speaking: This provides a visual record of who is speaking more than others.

Use of specific roles and processes to support group work

One of the difficulties for many children with group work is the unpredictable nature of the activity. They struggle to understand what they or others should do when working in a group. The social interaction demands are increased, as working in a group feels unpredictable and unstructured and so potentially unsafe. These anxieties can be reduced by attributing specific roles and processes in group work, providing a scaffold for the group task. Children may appreciate having a defined role and they can have the same role in future groups, if familiarity and repetition is helpful for them. For example: a child who can often dominate group discussions can be given the role of group spokesperson, curbing a potentially damaging behaviour and encouraging them to listen more.

Instead of this...	...try this
Provide each group in the class with a task and tell them to get on with it.	Identify the key features of the task for some, if not all of the groups. Set out clear roles for the different members of the group.

There is a range of literature on approaches to setting up groups and it is key to find something that works with your teaching style, the group of children with whom you are working and the task. As with most things in teaching, these approaches need to be adapted to be fit for the particular purpose. Here are some tips to help you navigate this.

Tip 1: Group roles

The basic idea is to allocate each child a specific role within the group, for example:

- chair, responsible for ensuring that everyone gets to speak
- record-keeper or scribe
- resource-gatherer
- spokesperson
- timekeeper.

These can be varied according to the task. Roles can be allocated at random and it is good to allow different children to experience different roles. However, we need to be aware of placing children in a position where their difficulties are shown up in a way that makes them vulnerable or increases anxiety. For example, it would not be appropriate to ask a child with significant literacy difficulties to act as the group's scribe.

There's a valuable metacognition element to the idea of roles: supporting children in thinking about their role, what it means and how they are going to do it. It sheds light on their interactions and makes them aware of their contributions. This is where group working becomes about 'learning to be in a group' and more overtly stretches beyond the confines of the subject matter.

Tip 2: Establish a process for group work

Again, there are many systems and approaches for supporting group work, including Edward de Bono's Six Thinking Hats (see www.debono.com) and Belle Wallace's TASC wheel (see www.tascwheel.co.uk). The key learning from these methodologies is the importance of a structure and a systematic approach to managing and tackling a task as a group. This makes group work easier to understand and follow for many children, including those with SEN.

It is very helpful to make these processes visual so that the whole group can see how they are working through the process and how they are moving from one stage to the next. This increases children's sense of control and understanding of the group and its working.

Tip 3: Supporting the engagement of all

As we have seen, there are many issues to ensuring that all children feel ready and confident to engage in group work and can do so effectively. But it is worth remembering that if a child is supported by now and next cards or visual prompts when working individually, they will continue to need these supports when working with others.

Tip 4: Use of space

Working space is always at a premium in schools and considering *how* to use space is key to making group work effective and supporting children to manage their sensory issues so they are able to engage with their group.

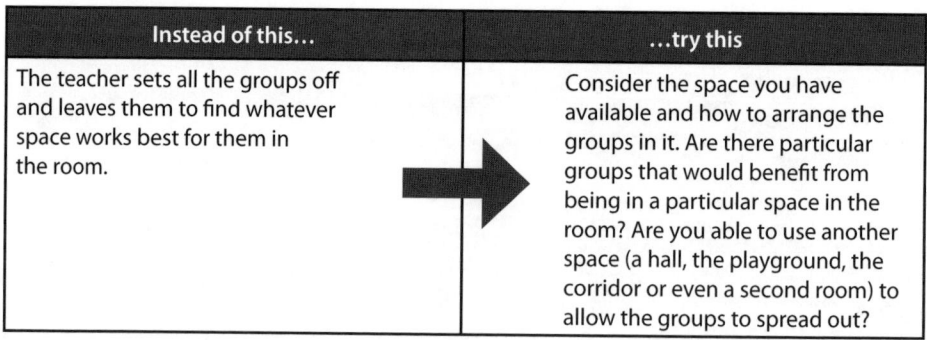

Instead of this...	...try this
The teacher sets all the groups off and leaves them to find whatever space works best for them in the room.	Consider the space you have available and how to arrange the groups in it. Are there particular groups that would benefit from being in a particular space in the room? Are you able to use another space (a hall, the playground, the corridor or even a second room) to allow the groups to spread out?

First, make sure you use all the space available. Where possible, plan your group work so the groups are able to spread out. Though moving furniture can create anxieties and sensory issues about change, it can create more space. If the groups are spread over a greater space, it reduces sensory issues.

Second, allocate the space carefully. Whatever space you end up using, allocate each group a space and be clear about the limits of their space. In this way, you can reduce conflicts arising from disputes over space between groups. As groups work, they will often spread, so they may need reminding where their working space begins and ends.

Some children may need support to consider how to share the space among themselves. We can minimise anxiety for children by talking them through how to use their allocated space. The more this is laid out, the more you create a structure to the activity, which can reduce the anxiety for children like Logan in our case study on page 116.

Sensory management

As soon as we move and change things in the classroom, which we do inevitably for group work, we impact children's sensory issues. These can act to distract children from learning and at times may become overwhelming and a barrier to learning. Often children are unaware of the real impacts of their sensory challenges. Then they may communicate their anxiety and discomfort through their behaviour and physical actions. We hope the following tips might help you to avoid this.

Tip 1: Pre-warn the children

As we have already said (and this really is a fundamental rule), children, particularly those who struggle with change, need routine to manage their anxieties. Arriving at the classroom to be faced with the unexpected can be challenging. Therefore, it is always worth warning children when group work activities are planned, so that the child comes to the lesson with an awareness of the expectations. If this is not possible, give them time to adjust to and process the expectations before you start the activity. Be prepared to allow for fidgeting and fiddling to support children to deal with any change of setting.

Think about this particularly if the lesson is happening somewhere different from the expected setting. We are all in favour of outdoor learning whenever possible, but we need to be aware that this opens up a whole new world of sensory stimulation and possible overload.

Tip 2: Focus on support for different sensory issues

Many children, particularly those with SEN, struggle to manage and regulate the messages from their different senses. At times, the range of sensory inputs can become overwhelming. When we work in groups in the classroom, we may be adding to these sensory challenges and need to consider how this may impact on children's ability to engage and learn.

Auditory

In a quiet classroom, a child with auditory processing difficulties can struggle to work out which of the many sounds to listen to and focus on. It can even be difficult to identify the teacher's voice from the sounds of children moving in their seats, the hum of the overhead projector, and noises from elsewhere in the building and outside.

We want to encourage and celebrate the beautiful sound of children learning with enthusiasm. However, something to balance with this is the problem that during group work noise levels can quickly rise, and even where only one person per group is talking, noise levels are likely to be greater than during normal classroom learning. Managing the noise level is key to supporting the successful engagement in group work for many children. Try the following:

- Make the expectations about noise levels explicit and stick to them. It is very easy to get distracted by the children's enthusiasm and not realise how noisy it is until a child has a meltdown or you have a headache.

- There are a number of online programmes that can be downloaded to display on an interactive whiteboard that show the level of noise in the classroom visually and act as a useful prompt to help the class manage their noise level.

- Consider support for individuals to help them manage noise levels, including use of ear defenders and opportunities for time out.

Visual

As children move around the room, it will change the visual impact and stimulation for children. Also, think about the way the task is presented and any possible impacts. Beware of children who have moved into the glare of an overhead projector or where resources such as mirrors, silver foil and torches may reflect light around the room.

Tactile

Often group work involves different or unusual materials being used; even things like flip chart sheets and marker pens can feel different and impact on children's sensory processing. It is worth considering the impact of any unusual materials – such as fabrics, polystyrene, wood and glue – being used. Any kind of messy activity involving paint, clay or cooking ingredients, even costumes in drama or sitting on the grass during outdoor learning, may impact a child with sensory issues.

Taste and smell

Anyone who has taught a group of pre-teenage boys immediately after PE is only too aware of smell in the classroom, yet outside of food technology we tend to disregard the impact of taste. It needs to be remembered how closely taste and smell are interlinked and the significant impact that they have on children's focus, concentration and wellbeing.

When children work in groups or even in pairs they work much more closely with others and this physical proximity will increase their awareness of bodily odours, good and bad. It should be remembered that for some the smell of perfume can be as difficult to manage as the smell of urine or vomit. Further, there are the smells related to resources being used. What to one person is the glorious smell of baking bread, to another person is sensory overload. We need to be aware of this, particularly in science, design technology, cooking and art and in spaces near where these activities are taking place.

Taste and smell are particularly difficult to manage as they are so personal, so a child may be responding to something about which we are completely unaware. Equally, a child may not be able to identify or articulate what is causing them the difficulty.

Proprioceptive and vestibular issues

Proprioceptive and vestibular issues (relating to the child's sense of balance and spatial awareness, including their sense of where their body is in relation to its surroundings) are the forgotten elements of sensory issues.

Group work provides great opportunities for children to work in different positions. Often, when working in groups, they end up standing, sitting on the floor or even lying down. Further, they may get the chance to work in different and more comfortable environments. However, the closer proximity of other people, the challenge of finding and maintaining an appropriate sitting position without wobbling into others and moving around a room where people are not where you expect them to be can all distract children from their learning.

Unfortunately, there are rarely quick fixes or obvious answers for helping children to manage their sensory issues. But starting with an awareness of what might be impacting on a child's focus and ability to engage can make a huge difference. It is part of the key process of thinking about what a child is communicating by their behaviour, so that you respond to the underlying cause of it, not just the visible behaviours.

Group size

We all know the saying that 'three's a crowd'. The larger the group, the more complex the social interactions involved. This means that it is better to start explicit teaching of group work skills with pairs and small groups and clearly structured activities. For those who have difficulties understanding and following social conventions, the simpler the context where they can practise their skills, the greater their chances of success. However, it should be remembered that one-to-one contexts bring particular pressures, such as eye contact and reduced thinking time to develop a verbal response when someone is waiting for a response only from you. When working in a group, others can model responses in ways that are not possible in a one-to-one interaction.

Further, it should be remembered that for many children there is an additional difficulty in 'generalising' the skills that they have developed in working one-to-one into a larger group setting. For these children, it is important to identify the skills they have developed and make an explicit link from one context to another to support the skills transfer.

Case study: Jo

Jo has poor speech and language skills, particularly in social communication. The staff supporting her have worked hard using barrier games and work with pictures to develop her skills to ask and answer simple questions. She has made good progress with this in the one-to-one intervention group but struggles to apply this when working in the classroom. Her teaching assistant is getting very frustrated with her. At the review with the SENCO, it was decided that Jo should practise using these skills in the intervention, working with another child who would then act as her partner in the classroom. Another child who would benefit from support in this area was identified. Through work in intervention groups and within the classroom, Jo developed her skills to work with this friend in a range of contexts.

Instead of this...	...try this
Stephan works hard and enjoys his LEGO® Therapy group. He has made excellent progress in asking questions and following others' instructions. Yet Stephan is still unable to work in a group in the classroom and you get cross with him. When you ask him why he doesn't use what he has learned in LEGO® Therapy, he looks at you blankly.	Stephan has been working on asking questions in his LEGO® Therapy group. This is supported by a series of visual prompts. Before Stephan starts working with a group in the classroom, he is reminded of what he has learned in his group and told that he is going to practise it in the classroom. He works with some of the children from his group. He has access to the same visual prompts he uses in the LEGO® Therapy group. When Stephan asks questions during the group work, he is given a sticker towards his reward time. The same rewards are used in the classroom. By doing this, Stephan is supported to make links between his learning in the intervention group and in the classroom.

Tip 1: Start small and structured

When looking to develop group work skills, start with smaller groups and move to larger groups slowly. Also focus on more structured tasks where the children can follow a clear structure to support them to work through the activity. It is always important to balance the social demands of working in a group and the academic demands of the learning, so choose the group size accordingly. Remember that not all the groups need to be the same size.

Tip 2: Put the children in groups before you give them the task

It is all too easy to tell children what they are going to do and then move them into groups. The problem with this is that nine times out of ten, by the time they are in the group, they will have forgotten what they were supposed to do. Of course, if you want them to choose their own groups on the basis of whom they will work with well to complete a particular task, they need to know the task first. Still, they will need reminding of the details before they start.

Tip 3: Provide a prompt for the task

Whatever the group size, it is always worth providing a written or visual prompt describing the task to remind the group of what they are supposed to be doing. If there are multiple stages for the task, it is worth creating a checklist of what children need to do for them to work through and refer to. Sometimes, the first job for the group can be to create the checklist. A verbal reminder of the task as they start work can also be helpful!

Working with a talk partner

In many schools, children have a regular 'talk partner', usually the person sitting next to them, with whom they share ideas about learning. For example, when the teacher asks a question as part of their input, the 'talk partners' can share their ideas. This enables children to:

- verbalise their thinking, supporting them to process and embed it
- formulate and practise their answers before sharing them with the class
- have the opportunity to share their ideas with someone even if they are not called upon to answer by the teacher
- engage with the learning, as they are required to talk to someone about it.

For children who struggle to work with others, all the issues that exist for group working in general exist in a microcosm for working with a talk partner.

Case study: Isaac

When Isaac was asked to talk to his partner, he would turn away as he hated making eye contact. When adults reminded him to talk to his partner, he would roll across the floor and under the nearest table, usually kicking someone en route. When he was fetched from under the table and taken back to sit by his partner, he usually hit them or the nearest adult. Not surprisingly, no one wanted to be partnered with Isaac and the adults in the room were beginning to feel it was easier to leave him under the table. So the school started to think about this differently; what was Isaac communicating? Firstly, Isaac didn't want to have to look directly at someone. In normal interactions, he was helped to understand that he didn't have to look at people unless he wanted to, as his teachers knew this caused him anxiety. Next, the school considered his relationship with his talk partner. They were confident that this was a child with whom Isaac wanted a connection as in other situations he interacted with them, talking, stroking their arm and bringing them objects – all clear signs of being in favour. It was then that the school began to focus on issues supporting turn-taking, beginning sentences and prompts for what to say. Over time, Isaac began to engage with his talk partner. It was a slow process that required ongoing support for both Isaac and his partner.

Instead of this...	...try this
You ask the class what they think will happen next in the story, then ask them to turn to talk to their partner while you check ahead in the book. Half of the children chat diligently to the person next to them about the story. The rest of the class is divided into those talking about something else, those staring into space, those making random noises, those hitting people and a pair in the corner with their hands up as they can't remember the question.	You stop reading and ask the children a question about the story. You record the question and symbol for paired talk on the board, so the children have it as a prompt. You move quickly to pick up the person whose partner is away and add them to another group. You check that those who need them have and are using their prompt cards. Then you sit with a pair to listen to and support their conversation.

As we have seen, having a regular talk partner is supportive for many children to help them formulate and practise sharing their ideas. Here are some thoughts about how to support the use of talk partners in your classroom.

Tip 1: Ensure everyone has a partner

It is very easy to say, 'Turn to the person next to you and discuss', but often this leaves someone on their own without a partner. It is much better for children to have pre-determined seating places that come with a set partner. With this approach, it is important to be aware of who is not in the room due to absence, being taught elsewhere or just going to the toilet, re-partnering children if necessary, even if this means creating a three.

Tip 2: Use prompts

It is very easy to assume that when asked to talk about something everyone will do it. But there is a range of issues where small tweaks can make this easier:

- For young children, by the time they have found their partner, they will have forgotten what they are doing. Even with older children (and adults), it is important to provide them with a reminder of the question.

- Support turn-taking; nominate a Red and a Green person in each group, with one speaking first, or use the idea of a speaking object mentioned on page 120.

- Many children struggle to know what to say. For many of them, the use of set sentences and learned scripts can be very supportive. For example, they can use sentence starters like: 'I think… because…'; 'It is right because…'; or 'Next we should…'. These can be shared with the whole class or used to support individuals or pairs. Where possible, it is helpful for these to be supported by visuals. It is often good for children to practise using these with an adult or in a highly structured activity, and then, once they are confident, move to using them in the whole-class setting.

- Use visuals. Many children find it easier to focus and remain on-topic if they have a visual to remind them of the subject of the conversation. For example, a picture of the story character they are discussing either on the board or right in front of the pair can support focus.

Tip 3: Consider timing

As with everything in teaching, timing for paired talk is key. But when we are searching for the magic moment to intervene and call a class back together again, it is important to remember that some children need longer to formulate, express and share their ideas and to understand and process what is said to them. Too often we pick our timing from the most able or the most potentially disruptive; we need to consider when to take the timing from those who need longer. Otherwise we are in danger of developing an exclusionist model where these children are never given an opportunity to finish paired talk tasks. It is a quick step from being stopped before you have time to finish a task to disengaging and never starting the task.

Tip 4: What to do with an additional adult

If you are lucky enough to have an additional adult in your classroom when you are using paired talk, it is very easy for them to become a barrier that inhibits the engagement of their focus child and their partner, by interpreting or interrupting interactions. If this happens, both the child and their peer may be discouraged from direct interaction as they will develop the expectation that an adult will mediate it. Adults have a hugely important role to play in supporting interactions such as paired talk, but it must be to support and not dominate or act as a child's mouthpiece.

When deploying another adult in the room during group work, it is important to consider:

- the focus of the activity: is this one that the child can meet without support?
- how much the child or children can be supported by working with their peers, so reducing the need for adult intervention
- what areas the child might find difficult and how to focus support on these rather than as an ongoing presence throughout the activity; an example would be allowing the child to work independently, but observing carefully and supporting time out to calm if they become anxious.

Sometimes the best way to support a child is to give them safe opportunities to work without support.

Monitoring and supporting groups

If group work is going well, a teacher can almost feel redundant. With group work, the teacher needs to frontload the process and focus on the preparation. If we get it right, group work can run itself. However, for many teachers this feels uncomfortable and disempowering. They want to be actively involved and in charge. The result is that we intervene, not always in a way that supports learning. For the majority of groups, only a light touch is needed. They will need praise, encouragement and recognition of their work, but they are able to progress and learn through the activity. There are some groups who will need more.

Case study: Zofia

As part of her tutor group's work for Safer Internet Day, Ms Musa organised her class into groups and asked them to produce a TV advert to promote internet safety. Her well-organised groups quickly started on the task. There was a cheerful buzz in the room and Ms Musa settled down to observe the groups. However, gradually it became clear that one group was struggling. There were raised voices and Zofia was sitting on the floor sulking. Ms Musa went over to try to support. Talking over each other, each child explained that no one was listening to their ideas. Ms Musa quietened them and reminded them of the structure of the activity and their group roles. Zofia was the chair, so she would choose who would speak and when. After some persuasion, Zofia returned to the group and the task. Ms Musa moved away, but kept a close eye on the group, intervening a few times with reminders about how to approach the task.

Instead of this...	...try this
You set your class off on a group work task, then visit each group in turn to check how they are getting on. However, you are aware that you are disturbing some groups and stopping the flow of their work, while others need your support and intervention more frequently.	You set the class off on a group work task. You give each group time to start; after observation of the groups, you visit them when they need support. Some groups need a lot of support while others need very little. You fit the support to the needs of the group.

As we have discussed, successful group work is not always easy, so here are some of our ideas to help facilitate it more successfully.

Tip 1: Give the group time

As adults in the classroom, we are always conscious of time. This means that all too often we rush children. We know from our own experiences that working in a group takes time to organise. We need to apply this to children and remember to give them time to work out their roles and relationships within the group. Working in groups takes longer, particularly at the beginning of a piece of work, and we need to plan and allow for this.

Tip 2: Let children attempt to solve issues before you get involved

This is always a difficult balance. You don't want groups or individuals to become overwhelmed, disheartened or disengaged, so it is very tempting to jump in to provide support for a group as soon as you identify that they are struggling or off-task. However, it is important to give children time to attempt to resolve issues themselves. This is part of the skills-building of group work and an important life skill. If we jump in too quickly, we build dependence on adults rather than allowing children to develop and practise their own skills.

Tip 3: Be aware that your presence or that of another adult changes the group

When you are working in a group and another person joins the group, particularly if they are in some way an authority, it changes the dynamic and interaction of the group. You might see it in CPD when staff are asked to discuss something in groups or pairs. As soon as the facilitator starts to listen in to a group, they change the way they work and at times even defer to the facilitator and seek approval for their ideas. The same is true for children. There are, of course, times when we want to use this to our advantage to refocus or redirect a group, but we need to be aware that we are changing the group's working and we should make a conscious choice about when and how to do it.

Feedback and sharing work

We have all been on a CPD course where we have gone around the room and had feedback from every group and by the time it has finished, we have lost the will to live. In the classroom it is key to balance this 'death by feedback' with the importance of recognising each group's working, allowing them to share and celebrate their work. The balance will depend on the class and the activity. But we need to be aware of disengaging children by either leading a sharing session that goes on for hours or leaving children feeling that their efforts have not been appreciated. This is particularly true when each group has completed the same task.

Teacher feedback and 'marking' are different issues and are the topics of another book. However, it is important that as teachers we demonstrate that we value the work children complete in groups, even where we do not formally 'mark' it. We also need to consider how we feed back on the work of a group and the individuals within it.

Tip 1: What is the feedback for?

When children are working in groups, we need to think about what we are giving feedback for, as there are two elements to the groups: the academic learning and the process of working in a group. Again, this is about considering the focus of the activity. But we need to remember that even if the focus is academic learning, children need feedback about their collaborative working skills. Feedback needs to both highlight and praise what children are doing well, on top of supporting areas of development. Much of this feedback should be part of the continuous process of monitoring and supporting groups.

Tip 2: Enable the groups to give each other feedback

There are many ways to divide the class so that they give feedback to other groups rather than to the whole class. They can then share what the other group did, if needed. Alternatively, representatives can visit another group to find out what they have learned and then return to their original group to share the new learning. It is worth considering opportunities for children to share their work with others beyond the classroom, including younger or older children, others working on the same topic in other classes, staff or parents.

Tip 3: Create an exhibition

This does not need to be a formal activity. It is simply a way to allow children to move around the classroom and see what other groups have done. This can be extended by allowing them to comment on a formal sheet or just on a whiteboard in front of the group's work.

Tip 4: Shape feedback around structured questions

As part of the structure of the activity, you can set up formal evaluation questions for the group to consider. Groups can focus on some or all of these questions. It is often useful to ask different groups to share their responses to different questions.

Alternatively, you can put each evaluation question on a separate sheet and then ask each group in turn to respond to one of the questions. Then pass the responses on to the next group, so that they have the opportunity to answer each question in turn, but also to see and respond to the other group's responses.

Tip 5: Ask the children to frame the evaluation in an interesting or different way

Ask the children to relate how they worked in the group to, say, an animal or a vegetable. A group could say that they worked like cheetahs as they worked really fast. Many children with special needs find this kind of non-literal thinking difficult, but others find it a good way to depersonalise feedback and talk about their learning in an unthreatening way.

Summary

Throughout this chapter, we have discussed the importance of using explicit roles and rules for group work to support all children to access it effectively. Implicit within this is the requirement for group work to be well-planned and the skills that support group work to be taught explicitly. Equally, there is a recognition that the ability to work effectively with others is a key life skill. The problem is, whose role is it to teach these skills? In a primary school, this responsibility can be laid at the door of the class teacher. But in secondary schools it is not so clear cut and all too easily it can fall down a gap and be taught by no one.

One of the key elements of effective group working is relationships and one of the most effective ways of teaching relationships is through modelling. The Nurture Group approach (see www.nurtureuk.org), developed from the work of Marjorie Boxall, supports children who have missed key development skills and attachment experiences that are prerequisite to learning. The approach regards the modelling of relationships by adults within the nurture group as key. It should be remembered that even where this kind of approach is not being followed, the relationships within school act as a constant model for the children. The children learn how to speak to each other, work together and manage conflict from the adults around them. These are key skills for successful group work.

The teaching of group work skills cannot be picked up by osmosis and observing others alone. It needs to be made explicit and discussed. For children to develop the skills and benefit from the strategies discussed above, they need to develop a degree of metacognition about working in a group. In this way, they will value and understand not just the academic learning element of the activity, but also the core social skills involved.

Identified issue	Suggestion/Check	My action	Any impact?
Do your groups include *all* children and enable them to feel like they belong?	How do you know?		
	How do you adapt your group work for learning different things?		
Inclusive groups checklist	Grouping children		
	Supporting turn-taking		
	Use of specific roles and processes to support group work		
	Sensory management		
	Group size		
	Working with a talk partner		
	Monitoring and supporting groups		
	Feedback and sharing work		

5 Phase 5 of the lesson: The last five minutes

'The end of your lesson is the beginning of someone else's. It's easy for a teacher to believe that you are only responsible for your own lesson, but children with a range of needs, and in fact the majority of children, see your lesson as part of the process of the day. In the child's mind, the lesson bell doesn't mean that it is all over; rather, it is a moment of transition through the journey of the day. The end of your lesson will have an impact on the next lesson.' Daniel Sobel

You have pulled off a fabulous lesson, and the child you are assessing appears to have been receptive and engaged. Having checked in a couple of times, you know they have achieved something valuable in the lesson. However, it's been 25 minutes since that last check-in and, if you are honest with yourself, you can't be confident that this child really understood what you have taught in the last half hour. You have a long list of thoroughly understandable reasons why you couldn't get back to this child to check in again with them and ascertain to what extent they were able to do the task effectively, or whether they really understood what they learned.

More importantly, it is difficult to assess where they are between the two completely different paradigms of: 1) What they have actually learned, and 2) What they think they have learned. This perception gap conundrum is what we as teachers are left with at the end of the lesson. This is especially true of the child who has cultivated the convincing nod and display of what appears to be meaningful activity, when in fact they are fine-tuning their (one day in the future Oscar-award-winning) acting skills (which is perhaps why so many famous actors struggled at school). This issue extends beyond the learning of the lesson you are just completing to the details of homework and what might be due by the next lesson – did they understand this? The reassurance that we give ourselves that this is the same routine we have been doing all year and therefore seemingly obvious is not foolproof for children who struggle with the routine and don't want to tell you they don't get it. There also will be a further group of children who don't realise that they don't get it.

The lesson is over, and the next hoard is about to barge into your domain for another 50 minutes, or maybe it's finally that toilet break you have been holding on for. The key goal is simply to get your current class out of the room on time – just get them out. In the melee, children with a variety of challenges experience something hidden and unnoticed. Consider the classroom exit for those with organisational challenges, sensory overload or proximity issues, those who don't know or can't remember what is coming next, the hyperactive students who use this opportunity to 'release' so their self-regulation goes out of the window, let alone the door, and any student with anxiety. The list could go on. The end of a lesson is not simple for many students with a wide range of needs.

This chapter attempts to uncover some of the elements that we miss in the last five minutes of the lesson because of the realities of the rush, the stress and the business of adhering to the regimen and time frame. We are focusing on this crucial yet often overlooked period and hope to share with you the simplest and most time-saving actions you can take to mitigate most, if not all, of these issues.

I remember my very first homework in secondary school. It is emblazoned on my memory for all the wrong reasons. I now know that the art teacher had asked us to use some drawing implements to show a colour spectrum from red to orange, then green, yellow and all the way through to blue. The problem was that when I was told to write it in my diary, I didn't know what to write. I didn't record the fact that it was due in two weeks' time. I didn't even know how to use this diary. When I arrived at the next lesson, I was one of three students who hadn't produced any homework, and I was told to stand up to be pointed out. I was embarrassed. After holding back tears and anxiety, I reassured the teacher that I would never commit this heinous crime again, and I would do the homework assignment by tomorrow morning on pain of death or, worse, a phone call to my mother to tell her how delinquent I was. I went home unsure of what to do and how to do it. I didn't know what to use: was it paints or pens or pencils? How big? On what?

After a late night with much anxiety, I ended up not doing it. The next morning, I asked a friend on the school bus how to do it, and realised that I didn't actually have any colours. I figured a single fountain pen colour on a strip of paper would do, and that led to my first lunchtime detention. After a few weeks I was pulled aside by one of the senior teachers who thought that I was a bit stupid, and asked whether this school was a good fit for me. A recurring feeling at the end of most lessons throughout my school experience was bewilderment, not knowing what the homework was and, even if I did manage to clarify it, not having an understanding of what was expected of me. Today, I have the best PA in the world, and she is quite used to telling me everything 12 times and helping me be organised with all of the specifics that I need. So, this chapter is quite close to home for me; some of the best SENCOs and senior leaders I have ever come across struggled at school, and this would have been fairly high up on their negative experience list, yet it is not something that gets much attention in the teaching fraternity.

Daniel

Child-led evaluation of learning

What did they *really* learn?

Self-evaluation is one of the many things that goes through fashions in education. It is rooted in the core questions: What does the child think they have learned? Can they identify this? How can they improve it? This is not a simple matter. For many children, when a piece of work is finished, it is finished. The idea of reviewing and evaluating the work seems odd and pointless. For others, it is just plain scary. It requires them to acknowledge that what they have done may not be perfect or admit that they had no idea what they were doing throughout an activity. Yet, as teachers, we constantly ask children to do this.

Case study: Szymon

At the end of the English lesson, the children are asked to edit their work. This becomes Szymon's cue to sharpen his pencil, go to the toilet, talk to his friends and generally practise his best work-avoidance strategies. Alternatively, he scans his work with a sense of desperation, unsure what he needs to do next. Clearly, he finds the task overwhelming. He has no idea what is meant by editing or how to approach the task. In order for Szymon to engage in effective editing, the task needs to be made smaller and more specific, so that he is able to focus on one thing at a time.

For too many children like Szymon, the concept of evaluation and editing is too complicated. It needs to be broken down into smaller, more explicit steps and modelled, so that they know exactly what the task entails. Children who experience difficulties with spelling, focus or concentration need an achievable goal and a clear purpose for what they are doing.

Instead of this...	...try this
You say to the whole class, 'Edit your work.' 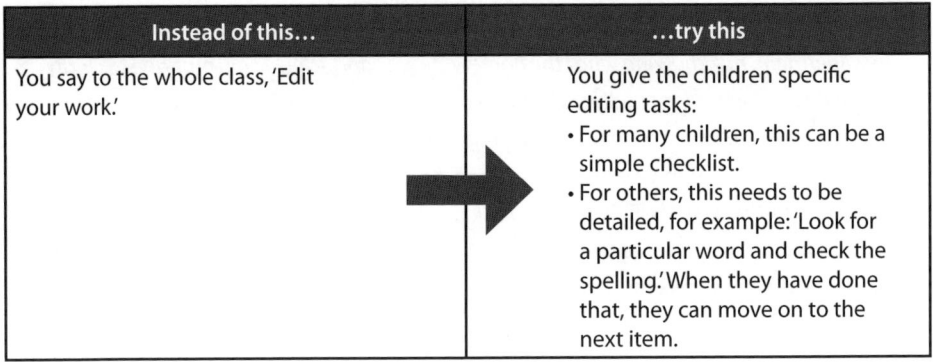	You give the children specific editing tasks: • For many children, this can be a simple checklist. • For others, this needs to be detailed, for example: 'Look for a particular word and check the spelling.' When they have done that, they can move on to the next item.

Top tips for supporting effective editing of work

As anyone who has attempted to write a book or even an essay knows, editing is not easy. When we reread our own work, we tend to read what we would have liked to have written rather than what we have written. Identifying errors and then correcting them, and, even more, extending and reframing ideas are difficult. Yet, it is something that we expect children to attempt from the first time they start to write. Here are some simple ideas to support and ease this process.

- Working with a 'critical friend': Instead of asking a child to reread their own work, ask them to work in pairs and read their work to each other. As we have said, when we read our own work, we tend to read what we hope we have written. However, when we hear it aloud, it is easier to register what is actually on the paper and to identify what needs to be edited. Also, the 'critical friend' can share and discuss ideas and give the reader's point of view of the text.

- The 'read aloud' feature on many word processing programmes also allows the child to hear their work read aloud, supporting them to identify errors. For the latter to be used effectively in the classroom, it depends on the child's work being typed in the first place and having access to headphones, so that their work is not shared with the whole class. The impact can be reduced by the idiosyncratic pronunciation of the computer programme.

- 'Focused editing': For children who struggle to identify spelling errors, particularly those who may spell the same word several different ways within the same piece of writing, identify a maximum of three words, ideally words that they have used several times. Show them the word in writing and ask them to find every time they have used the word and then circle it. Once they have done this, they should tick it if it is correctly spelled, and correct it if it is not. Once they have embedded these words, they move on to a new group of words.

- Peer evaluation: Have clear rules for peer evaluation so the children are enabled to look constructively at each other's work with a purpose in mind. There should be a clear focus to identify exactly what the children are looking for, as well as rules about how to work together, for example, not to write on each other's work. This process needs to be scaffolded. Many children find a bank of sentence stems useful, such as:
  - I like how you described…
  - The punctuation… could be changed to…
  - This is not quite clear because…
  - Why did you use the word…?
- Consider the use of IT for children to photograph or record their work. They can then comment on either their own or each other's work.

What did I *really* learn?

At the beginning of the lesson, most teachers have some form of learning intention or objective, supported by a success criterion. This may be stated or unstated. When the learning objective is shared with the children, it is questionable how far it actually impinges on their consciousness. We know many children who copy 'learning intentions' directly into their books without considering the words they are writing. It can become the classic example of passing from the notes of the teacher to the notes of the student without passing through the mind of either. Alternatively, the learning intention and success criteria may become an administrative nightmare tightly bound to school requirements, to the extent that teachers worry so much about getting it exactly 'right' that it ends up having little to do with the individual lesson or child's learning.

For many children, it is difficult to separate what they have done and what they have learned. They might say, 'I've done maths' or 'I have used cubes' instead of 'I've learned to add three-digit numbers.' This is because they are not able to identify their learning; it is too vague. They do not understand which part is the learning; the process of engaging with skills or knowledge so that you can use and apply them later or in a different context is a concept that is too complex for them. Understanding when and how this process is happening is difficult for teachers and so much more so for children, and in particular those with special needs. Many learning intentions or objectives shared with children are a mixture of what the children should do and the expectation of what they will learn. The issue is further confused by what the teacher is 'teaching' and what the child is actually 'learning'. We suspect that part of the problem is that it is difficult for teachers and school leaders to separate and identify 'teaching', 'learning' and 'doing'.

Further issues make children's self-evaluation more difficult, including:

- difficulties understanding the teacher's expectations
- a feeling that they are being asked to focus on the things that their special needs make particularly difficult for them, such as spelling or handwriting, which compounds their sense of failure.

Case study: Yasmin

Yasmin is an able and motivated child, whose design technology teacher complained that she refused to evaluate her work effectively, and often wrote something pointless or sarcastic. Through discussions with Yasmin, the problem quickly became clear. She knew what she needed to improve, but she was also aware of what she found difficult. She was very aware that her physical and coordination skills prevented improvement in those areas (for example, being able to draw a straight line). Recording these challenges compounded her sense of failure, so she chose to opt out. She needed support to see the evaluation process in a different way, so that she would be able to identify what she had done well and tasks that she would be capable of improving.

How can we make the process of self-evaluation useful and supportive of learning? There are many books and articles written on this topic, and in this short book we cannot hope to capture or summarise all of the research. We will, however, highlight that children are supported in many ways by knowing what they are going to learn, and in order to evaluate their learning effectively, this process needs to be explicitly taught. If children don't know what they have learned, they can't evaluate it. This is supported by clearly defining what we want the children to evaluate, for example:

- working through a checklist
- evaluation in response to specific questions
- focusing children to look at specific items
- giving children a scale to evaluate their work

- considering the effort they feel they made, rather than solely what they achieved
- giving an example with which to compare their work.

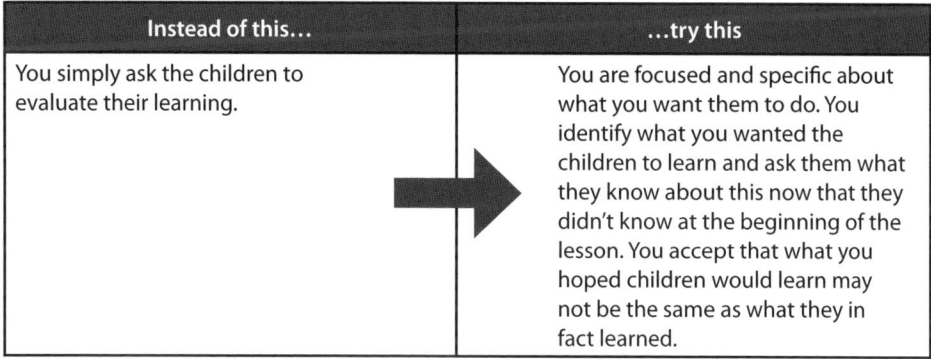

Instead of this...	...try this
You simply ask the children to evaluate their learning.	You are focused and specific about what you want them to do. You identify what you wanted the children to learn and ask them what they know about this now that they didn't know at the beginning of the lesson. You accept that what you hoped children would learn may not be the same as what they in fact learned.

Fundamental to the effective use of evaluation is 'metacognition' – developing an understanding of how we learn and what helps us to learn effectively. This is another of those vast areas of educational theory where numerous books have been written. We are not going to attempt to recap all the research, discussions and arguments. Metacognition is discussed briefly on page 22.

Teacher-led evaluation of the child's learning

How do you (the teacher) know what the child has actually learned?

The teacher's evaluation goes hand in hand with the child's editing and evaluation of their work and learning. This is key to effective teaching. We cannot teach effectively unless we are clear what the children know and are learning, so that we can identify gaps and misconceptions. Equally, we need to share our own evaluations (comments and marking) with the children in a way that supports their understanding that evaluating and reviewing their own work is a useful and worthwhile activity.

We need to develop evaluations that focus on what the child has done well and is able to improve, rather than merely acting as a reminder of what they struggle with. If we only focus on the challenging aspects, we build a feeling of annoyance and resentment in the child and compound a sense of failure, leading to disengagement with learning.

> *I still remember the sinking feeling as I looked at every piece of English work I ever did at school and saw the list of words, often more than 30 of them, that I had misspelled and had to copy out three times. It was a pointless activity. I continued to misspell them, and they were the same words again and again. Both my teacher and I knew it was a pointless activity that had no positive impact on my spelling. Not only did it have no positive impact but it also had a significant negative impact. It fed into my feeling that I couldn't write and was useless at English. This was not something for the likes of me. I gave up English as soon as I was allowed, and it took me nearly 40 years (and the development of word processing software with spell checks) before I felt confident to write anything again.*
>
> *Sara*

Many schools have learned something about marking since we were at secondary school and have begun to move beyond the old standby of 'improve your handwriting.' Yet so much of marking gets caught up with school protocols and policies that the direct link between teaching, evaluation and the child's learning gets lost.

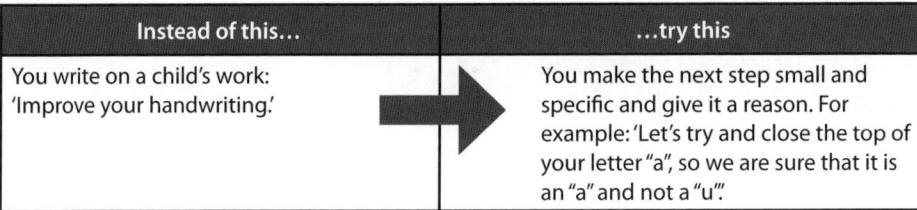

Instead of this...	...try this
You write on a child's work: 'Improve your handwriting.'	You make the next step small and specific and give it a reason. For example: 'Let's try and close the top of your letter "a", so we are sure that it is an "a" and not a "u".'

There is a current trend for verbal feedback, which is great and has huge potential to create evaluation and feedback as valuable communication between the teacher and child. Verbal feedback also reduces teacher workload and eradicates marking just for the sake of showing that you have marked the book. We do need to be aware, however, that the children may not remember verbal feedback, and therefore may not be able to act on it. Further, what you tell them about their work may not be what they hear or understand. How often have you been given feedback on your teaching and only remembered the negatives? If we ask a child to look again at Question 7 because they got it wrong, they will only focus on that and not fully register that this means they got nine out of ten questions right.

Schools often make the assumption that what a child has learned is only evidenced by what appears in their book. This is where the overall evaluation of what a child has learned in a lesson goes far beyond what is recorded in a book (and that is without even considering lessons such as PE, drama and music). This still leaves us with the question, as teachers, of how we know what the child has learned. This is why we so often fall back on assessing what we have taught, because it is easier to identify.

The perception gap conundrum

This is where we hit the perception gap: the gap between what the teacher believes they have taught and what the child has learned, compared with what the child understands and tells you they have learned. We, as teachers, are used to simply asking the child whether they understood, whether they have completed the task and so on. We do this in many ways: thumbs up, putting your books in different-coloured piles, writing self-evaluation statements and so on. Many of these can be useful and effective but, like any opinion poll, we need to be aware that the information given is only as good as the question asked. A number of respondents will misunderstand the question, and some will simply lie, while yet others will respond that they understood and have learned what is expected because they genuinely believe that they have. Indeed, they may have understood the lesson up to the point at which the teacher asks, but just ten minutes later they are lost.

Case study: Ethan

Teachers always commented that Ethan was 'a sweetie, always smiling'. Indeed he was, and at the end of every lesson he was the first to stick his thumb up to indicate that he had understood what had been taught and he would be able to use and apply his learning in the next lesson. On this evidence, Ethan was doing well. In reality, it took only a single focused question or a glance at his book to see that this was not the case. Ethan was working several years behind his classmates in all areas of the curriculum. His confident smile and his belief that he could access the learning belied his complete lack of understanding of it.

Ethan was an extreme example of the child who does not understand what they are supposed to have learned. There are others who, as we have already discussed, struggle to distinguish between learning and doing. The perception gap goes beyond the gap between teaching and learning. This gap between what is taught and what children are able to apply and reshape for themselves, in a range of contexts, goes directly to the heart of the educational process.

Case study: Laurette

At the end of every lesson, when the class was asked to evaluate and consider their learning, Laurette always put up her hand and was ready to offer a response. Her teacher resisted calling on her, as Laurette's answer was usually long, convoluted and irrelevant. The teacher finally understood that Laurette was attempting to answer the question very literally by telling the class *all* that she had learned. However, there was a complete mismatch between what Laurette said and what the teacher wanted the class to learn. Two issues were causing this: firstly, Laurette had not fully understood the point and focus of the lesson at the beginning of the session; secondly, she lacked the skills or understanding to identify what she had learned and to separate this from the simple recollection of the activities she had carried out. In answer to the question, 'What did you learn?', Laurette might reply, 'I used these three cubes and put them together and then I took some more cubes and added them too…'. At no point could she identify any specific aspect that she had learned.

Laurette did not understand the learning and was not able to explain what she had learned. There are others who can understand the learning when it is freshly taught but will struggle to retain and recall it later, or who can repeat it in that particular context, setting and situation, but will struggle to apply and use their learning independently. For these children there is a gap between what is taught and what has been learned.

Case study: Elijah

Elijah has little or no communicative intent and very significant social communication difficulties. He will echo what others have said around him, but without understanding the context or meaning. In school, his teachers are working hard on developing his vocabulary for naming everyday objects and key verbs to describe actions using visual and physical prompts. His mum has worked on developing his phonic knowledge and he is now able to blend a series of three and occasionally four phonemes to create a word. He is able to read 'dog' or 'cat' using phonics. This would suggest that he is learning to read. However, while Elijah is able to read both 'dog' and 'god', he is not able to differentiate that one set of sounds represents a furry barking animal and the other a deity. Both are a meaningless set of sounds that he can mechanically make in response to a set of symbols.

Instead of this...	...try this
You quickly scan the room and ask the most able children to explain what they have learned, hoping that one of them will produce something that matches the learning intention shared at the beginning of the lesson. Hearing the desired answer, you breathe a sigh of relief and assume all the children have understood the learning.	During the lesson, you move around the room and talk to the children about their learning, intervening to support them as you go. You guide them to comment on their learning, then use these comments as part of the plenary at the end of the lesson and see how far other children agree with them.

To avoid the perception gap, think carefully about the following:

- Exam checking: Too often, when we ask children to check their work, particularly in exams and other assessments, they only look at the answers and don't reread the questions. They need support to understand the link between the question and the answer, and that the answer needs to relate to the question.

- Whole-class praise: Consider the impact of saying, 'Well done! You can all now do…' or 'We have all learned to…' For any child who feels they can't do whatever the class is being praised for, this is a form of public shaming. It can have a significant impact on their self-esteem and engagement.

- What *has* been learned: Children may not have learned what we originally intended in a lesson, but that does not necessarily mean that they have learned nothing of value.

Leaving the room and transitioning

We are all aware that a good routine encourages a calm start to our lesson (and if not, may we respectfully suggest you revisit Chapter 1 of this book!). However, we are often less focused on good routines at the end of the lesson. The issues arising from the disorganised end of a lesson, where everyone grabs their equipment, gets up and pushes their way out, not only impact on the next lesson as we have discussed, but actually leak into your own lesson. As you start your plenary and finish up the lesson, there will be children who have already disengaged. Their anxieties will be ramping up. They will be anticipating the chaos, sensory overload and difficulties to be unleashed upon them with the lesson bell. The thought of managing the sensory overload of the noise and movement of the school corridor, the fear of unkind remarks, losing their belongings and maybe even losing their way become so overwhelming that the last ten minutes of the lesson are lost to a rising sense of panic. How we end the lesson impacts our lesson as well as the next one.

We often forget not only the impact of the end of the lesson, but also the impact that the journey to and from lessons can have as well.

> *I remember my first visit to a secondary school as a newly pregnant advisory teacher in the early 1990s and being caught in a corridor during a lesson change. I was so terrified that I hid in the nearest toilets; luckily, it was a staff toilet, less luckily, it was for male staff. However, I doubt my feelings of sensory overload and fear of being squashed in the stampede were unique, and even though things have improved, there will be children who feel like this today.*
>
> *Sara*

Case study: Freddie

Freddie always bounces into the class as a hyperactive ball of enthusiasm and lost possessions. With support, he settles quickly into the class routine and for about two-thirds of the lesson he engages well and tries hard. He loves praise and benefits from regular adult check-ins. However, as soon as you introduce any kind of plenary or learning summary, Freddie begins to lose it. He starts shouting out, fidgeting and leaving his seat. His normal disorganised pile of belongings – books for other lessons, his pencil case, the odd trainer that has found its way onto his desk – becomes overwhelming and starts to impinge on other children's space, disrupting them and Freddie.

For Freddie, the last five or ten minutes of the lesson are not about finishing that lesson; he is already thinking about moving on to the next. For him, this is a cause of almost overwhelming anxiety. In order to attempt to maintain focus, Freddie needs to know what is happening and to have a secure routine for both the end of the lesson and the transition to the next. Only by clearly setting this out for him can we hope for him to engage in the end or beginning of any lesson.

Instead of this...	...try this
You rush through your plenary, finishing two or three minutes after the bell has gone and leaving the children negative time to get to the next lesson without being late.	You give the children time checks and use them to ensure that the lesson finishes punctually, so that no one is anxious that they are going to be late for the next lesson or, even worse, lunch. You finish your lesson using a calm and planned routine so that the children know what to expect.

Top tips for successful end-of-lesson routines

It is funny how much emphasis is put on the beginning of a lesson compared with the end. Yet both are equally important to children's success in the learning and are supported by establishing clear and effective routines. Here are a few of our tips for routines to use at the end of lessons.

Tip 1: Use pre-warnings

We all know how irritating it is when we are asked to stop something in the middle. Yet we do this all the time to children.

Case study: Adnan

Adnan is very able, but suffers from a significant level of anxiety, particularly about writing. This paralyses him, so that he is unable to engage in any activity involving writing. It becomes clear over time that one of the many issues is his feeling that as soon as he has an idea and starts to write, he will be interrupted and stopped, so it is not worth starting.

Instead of this...	...try this
You say, 'Pens down. Finish what you are doing.'	You give the children time warnings, so they know when they will be expected to finish a task.

Most parents know the importance of giving pre-warnings to children: 'Five minutes until bedtime,' 'Five minutes and we are going home.' This is part of the daily life of a parent. Yet we do not always use this strategy in our classrooms, particularly as the children get older. We expect them to monitor the time themselves, or we just expect the children to stop when asked. By pre-warning children towards the end of the task, we enable them to prepare for a smooth transition.

Pre-warnings and time checks can be supported by a visual to indicate that the end of the lesson or task is coming. There are many useful timers that can be displayed on interactive whiteboards to show the countdown to the end of any activity. However, we need to be aware that for many children with sensory issues these can become overwhelming and a source of anxiety too. In addition, children can become transfixed by watching the timer so that they are unable to engage with any learning. With this in mind, these resources need to be used carefully.

Tip 2: Have clear task endings

We often tell children to 'finish their work'. This instruction carries with it the implication that the child knows what this means. Does it mean to finish the sum, the page of sums or everything on the board? This issue is further complicated when we ask children to finish their work, but they are in fact working on a task that will be carried on the next day or in the next lesson. In this case, we need to be clear what we mean by 'finished for today'. This is a particular issue for some children as they move from reading short books that can be completed in a single sitting to reading longer books that are completed over days or even weeks.

For most tasks, the expected finished result is flexible. Writing for 20 minutes will look different for different children, and indeed for the same child on different days. Most children can manage this degree of uncertainty, but not all. The majority of children benefit from understanding the teacher's expectation of the finished activity. For some, clarifying this expectation is essential, as without this support they cannot start the task, let alone finish it. This can be a modelled example or clear instruction, such as: 'Complete ten sums,' or 'Write to here,' shown by a mark on the page, and so on. Children need to know what 'finished' looks like before they can be certain that they have finished.

Tip 3: Ensure that finished means finished

Setting a clear end to a task can be more complex than it first appears. When we set out a clear expectation for a task, but a child finishes before the end of the lesson, it is all too tempting to add an extension task. Often this is the right thing to do. But for those children who are highly routine- or rule-bound, this creates confusion. For others, it tells them that if they complete their work they will just get more, so it is better not to complete the work. To counter this, we need to be clear what our expectations are, or the unexpected presentation of an extension task can feel like a punishment and become a disincentive to complete the task.

Tip 4: Use tidying up as a learning experience

In Early Years classrooms, tidying up is explicitly taught. The teacher will establish specific routines, often with a musical accompaniment to encourage engagement and support understanding of the routine. As children get older, tidying up becomes an expectation, but it is rarely explained. We issue instructions: 'Put your books away', 'Pick up the paper', 'Straighten the chairs'. We expect the children to follow. Most children have enough experience from home or elsewhere to be able to generalise these instructions and apply them to the classroom setting. Others have the skills and understanding to follow the modelling of those who get it. But some will remain disengaged and confused. They remain apart from the activity or engage in meaningless 'busyness' to cover up the fact that they are not sure what is expected of them. These children need the tidying up to be modelled, and often to be given specific tasks as they would in the rest of the lesson, so that they can engage.

For many children with sensory issues, tidying up at the end of the lesson can be used as a specific opportunity to support them. For example, for children with proprioceptive needs, tidying up can enable them to engage in the 'heavy load' work, such as moving chairs, books or other equipment, that helps to manage their sensory needs. For others, the movement break of collecting resources will enable them to be calm and refocused before they leave the room.

Tip 5: Plan end-of-lesson routines

Exactly what the finishing routine will be depends on the lesson and the age of the children, but what is clear is that it needs attention. The following should be included at some level:

- support for ensuring children have their belongings and are organised to be able to pack them into their bags appropriately; if necessary, some may need support to carry them
- support to help children manage anxiety and sensory overload
- a clear and planned route to help the children reach their next lesson safely and within the time limit.

Tip 6: Mark the stages of the lesson

As we've mentioned, Reception, and sometimes infant school classes, often use 'tidy up music', which is played at the end of the lesson to gently remind children to finish what they are doing and encourage them to tidy up. It provides a clear auditory cue and support for transition. But many children need this kind of support long after we stop using it. We need to consider age-appropriate ways of using visual and auditory signs to mark the stages of the lesson, so not only is the lesson end clear, but the journey through the lesson is clear as well.

Consider the use of a marker on lesson slides to display this. For example:

Starting activities → Teacher input → Group activities → Individual learning → Summing up and plenary

Tip 7: Be aware of particular anxiety points

For some children, particular times of day or week may be triggers for increased anxiety. Many children (and adults!) begin to struggle as they move towards lunchtime. For many, as they become hungry, particularly if this is combined with anxieties such as managing lunch routines, having sufficient time to eat, finding a food choice they like or bullying from others, their ability to manage the end of the lesson successfully will be reduced.

Equally, as we approach home-time, anxiety can increase. For primary school children, there can be anxieties about being picked up or managing the transition into an after-school activity. As children become older, there may be anxieties about the journey home and managing interactions with others as they leave the safe environment of the school. For children dependent on school or public transport, there are concerns about missing the bus or train and what might happen on that journey.

There will be multiple other times in the school day or week that act as triggers for anxiety for particular individuals – specific lessons, interactions with certain staff or peers, or going into different areas of the school building. We need to be cognisant of these anxieties and enable children to share them, so that we can support the children to manage and hopefully reduce their anxieties.

Often, we will need to keep records of incidents and concerns to help us identify and act on these triggers, as otherwise neither staff nor the children will be explicitly aware of the anxiety points or able to act to reduce their impacts.

Tip 8: Think flexibly

In many schools, the support for children with special needs is focused on support for learning and is therefore based in lessons. This is particularly true in secondary schools where the support is organised in faculties or departments. This means that children with physical and sensory issues, social communication difficulties or mental health and anxiety issues are left to negotiate lesson transitions unsupported. For many of these children, transition times are the most difficult part of the day. The structured lessons are easier for them to manage than the unstructured transitions and breaks. When we are allocating SEN support, it may be worth considering whether giving the children more support to navigate unstructured times would reduce their anxiety and enable them to access learning with greater independence. For example, maybe some children would benefit from a staggered start or end for lessons, so that they have more time to move from place to place or are able to make the journey in quieter corridors.

The emotional impact of the lesson

You've probably heard the quotation, 'At the end of the day people won't remember what you said or did, but they will remember how you made them feel.' Although the source of this is unknown, the message is clear, and this is key to having a successful lesson ending.

> *While working with a school to support a girl who was at very high risk of exclusion, I asked the girl to tell me something that was good about school. Her answer was 'science'. She was not willing or able to say why she liked science or what was good about it. Later, in conversation with the head of science, this girl's name cropped up. The teacher lit up and talked about the girl with real enthusiasm and love. She didn't deny her difficulties, or the challenges of having her in a room with other children, but the fact that she loved and valued this girl was clear. The child knew and felt this, which contributed to her enjoying science lessons. This enabled us to build a starting point to help this girl return to classes.*
>
> *Sara*

When a child is able to carry the feeling that they are valued and wanted from one lesson to the next, it helps them to manage the transitions. For many children, there is a real need to extend the belief that their teacher likes them and believes in them. When they are able to take this knowledge beyond the classroom, it can give them security and a sense of belonging, thus enabling them to manage transitions successfully.

Summary

'Learning' is generally discussed in a formal manner, but it is so much more than picking up curriculum points – it is an all-encompassing part of life and the whole experience of school. Arguably, these may well be the most important lessons that children will carry with them throughout their lives – and we bet not one was ever written on a lesson plan. Encourage and praise learning of all kinds, especially learning that arises from unexpected incidents and problems that emerge. It is likely that children will learn more from you about how you react to the unpredictable than whatever it is you lay out in a predictable format. This is not about you being perfect or pretending to always be unruffled; sometimes it's about being honest with children that you are a human being and make mistakes too.

We've considered the idea that children may well be thinking about the next lesson or lunch break. It's natural to worry ahead, to be thinking about what's coming up. This is probably a simple survival skill. The idea then that we all – teacher and child alike – can focus 100 per cent until the end of the lesson is probably deluded. Far better to embrace it, and construct an ending process that addresses this reality, rather than attempting to avoid the inevitable.

Identified issue	Suggestion/Check	My action	Any impact?
Child-led evaluation of learning	How does the child communicate with you about what they have learned?		
What did I *really* learn?	How do you (the teacher) know what the child has actually learned?		
	Does the evidence of the children's learning match the teacher's expectations?		
Successful end-of-lesson routines	Is the end of class predictable and doable for *all* children?		
	Is leaving the room and transitioning thought through?		
	What is the emotional impact of the lesson ending?		

Putting it all together

Of course, things will always go wrong. You can plan to your heart's content, but any experienced teacher will tell you that you need to be able to think on your feet. So, instead of sticking rigidly to the structure of the phases we have outlined and allowing things to blow up into big issues that may lead to a child exiting the classroom, use the adaptations we have shared and be willing to be flexible. In other words, routines throughout the five phases are best, but only if you can adapt them when necessary. If there is a fire, then exit the classroom. If a child is becoming violent, then you need to remove the other children from the classroom.

Establish simple and consistent routines and apply small tweaks and adaptations to meet individual children's needs. Key to this is remembering that both children and situations change, so we will constantly need to be aware that what worked last week may not work this week. Therefore, we will need to tweak or adapt again. It is this process that is at the heart of successful and effective inclusive teaching. We hope that because the tweaks and adaptations are small, they will not be overly stressful for teachers to implement or children to understand.

Let's recap what we have shared in a visual synopsis so that you can see how it all comes together.

PHASE 1: TRANSITION, ENTERING THE CLASSROOM AND PREPARING TO LEARN	**Aim:** Starting the lesson calmly.
	How: Be warm and welcoming, establish clear routines and build confidence and self-belief.
	• Warmly greet the children. • Think about who comes into the room when. • Support children with particular roles. • Have an effective seating plan: think about sitting – where and how. • Prepare equipment and materials needed and use lots of visuals. • Use your room to promote positivity. • Pre-warn of change and use a range of resources and strategies to help manage change. • Use pre-learning.

PHASE 2: DELIVERING AND RECEIVING INSTRUCTIONS AND WHOLE-CLASS ENGAGEMENT

Aim: Communication to be understood by *all*.

How: Use simple, reiterated instructions and check to see if children understand.

- Simplify your instructions and ensure their focus is clear.
- Use visual, written, non-verbal instructions to support your message.
- Encourage and enable children to ask questions.
- Don't ever assume the child has understood.
- Know that children will miscommunicate to you too.
- Allow thinking time and rehearsal.
- Match the activity and the child's ability.
- Utilise different ways for children to share their views and participate.

PHASE 3: INDIVIDUALS WORKING AS A CLASS

Aim: Enabling children to participate independently.

How: Differentiate, prompt, praise and vary approaches.

- Prioritise learning over admin and think before asking children to copy.
- Differentiate by support, process, outcome and assessment.
- Use different ways for children to share, show and record their learning, including IT.
- Embed assessment adaptions into classroom practice.
- Teach note-taking, self-talk for learning and classroom skills.
- Support starting tasks and make endings clear.
- Consider the impact of classroom noise and sensory issues.

PHASE 4: INDIVIDUALS FITTING INTO A GROUP OF LEARNERS

Aim: Groups that are places of belonging for all and that promote and extend learning while developing key social skills.

How: Plan, use routines, assign roles, promote self-esteem, and reward participation and inclusivity.

- Make the routines explicit and provide prompts to support them.
- Be flexible with your groupings and change them to fit the activity.
- Use our 'group work toolkit'.
- Balance academic and social demands.
- Start group work with children's strengths.
- Give explicit praise for groups enabling *all* children.
- Prompt for turn-taking and sharing ideas.
- Check to see if key students are participating.

PHASE 5: THE LAST FIVE MINUTES

Aim: An ending to the lesson that will fully prepare and enable *all* students to engage in the next activity.

How: Be warm and encouraging, establish clear routines, and build confidence and self-belief.

- Consider not only what the child has learned, but what they believe they have learned.
- Check if what children have learned and what they have done are different.
- Warmly encourage the children.
- Think how you pack up the room and who you ask to help.
- Support children with particular roles.
- Use your room to promote positivity.
- Pre-warn of change and use a range of resources and strategies to help manage change.
- Use after-learning.
- Remember your lesson is only one phase of the child's day.

Communication

If you are setting up routines, adaptions and tweaks in your classroom, it is important that these are consistent. In order for them to be consistent, they must be shared. This means that the TAs or other adults in the room should be aware of them and understand why they are being implemented. Equally, others who come into the room – PPA, cover and supply teachers – need to know the shared expectations in the room. One of the biggest issues with implementing anything within schools is consistency. Let's be clear: we do not think that everything in every classroom should be the same. Quite the contrary: teachers should be making constant adaptions to meet the needs of their children. But the expectations within the room should be about consistency and this should be communicated, so that children are not faced with the anxiety of trying to second-guess how things will change when someone different is in the room. The change alone is enough stress for many children.

Equally, it is important to listen to and share with the children. One of the current buzz phrases in many areas is 'co-production': the importance of involving, listening to and sharing with clients, patients and participants when developing plans and structures to support them and meet their needs. As teachers, we need to remember that we are only a small part of the classroom ecosystem, and to create a sustainable environment, we need to consider the needs of all the inhabitants. As part of this process, teachers need to listen to the children, so that they can respond to their needs. It is very easy to forget that the children may have ideas about how best to support their needs, even if they are not able articulate them in 'teacher speak'.

Final thoughts

Our final thoughts are that much of this work can be implemented effectively within the individual classroom, but each classroom is set within the school, and the ethos, culture and atmosphere of the whole school impacts on what happens within each classroom. As we emphasise in the sections on both Phase 1 and Phase 5, no lesson stands alone. The beginning and end of your lesson are the connection to other lessons, other parts of the school day and the transition in and out of school. They will impact on and be impacted by these outside influences. To be most effective, your routines and adaptions will need to fit within the wider approach of the whole school. We hope that the approach to differentiation laid out in our book can be shared across schools and beyond, so that it can make the most difference to the children we teach.

May your work be recognised and praised.
May you be encouraged and celebrated for your efforts.

May you touch the life of one child and give them opportunities and hope where perhaps no other teacher was able to.

It is one of the most noble endeavours that we humans can do – to be a teacher. We know the complexity, skill and sophistication it takes. Without your (often overly) hard work and dedication, passion and belief in your children, our profession and our most vulnerable children will succumb to 'datafication', box-ticking and financial constraints.

It is our dream and hope that inclusion will evolve to a new epoch, where it is no longer something that we have to do as an extra but something that has evolved to be part of the everyday norm, to the extent that we no longer notice it. In so doing, we believe that it will support not only children, but also teacher wellbeing.

References

Bergland, C. (2014), 'Tackling the "vocabulary gap" between rich and poor children', *Psychology Today*, www.psychologytoday.com/gb/blog/the-athletes-way/201402/tackling-the-vocabulary-gap-between-rich-and-poor-children

Bombèr, L. M. (2007), *Inside I'm Hurting*. London: Worth Publishing.

Bryan, K., Freer, J. and Furlong, C. (2007), 'Language and communication difficulties in juvenile offenders', *International Journal of Language and Communication Disorders*, 42, (5), 505–520.

Campbell, P. H., Milbourne, S. A. and Silverman, C. (2001), 'Strengths-based child portfolios: a professional development activity to alter perspectives of children with special needs', *Topics in Early Childhood Special Education*, 21, (3), 152–161.

Cheng, J. (undated), 'Just a label? Some pros and cons of formal diagnoses of children', http://smhp.psych.ucla.edu/pdfdocs/diaglabel.pdf

Clanchy, K. (2019), *Some Kids I Taught and What They Taught Me*. London: Picador.

Department for Education (2013), 'National curriculum in England: English programmes of study', www.gov.uk/government/publications/national-curriculum-in-england-english-programmes-of-study

Department for Education (2018), 'Permanent and fixed-period exclusions in England: 2016 to 2017', www.gov.uk/government/statistics/permanent-and-fixed-period-exclusions-in-england-2016-to-2017

Department for Education (2020), 'Statistics: school workforce', www.gov.uk/government/collections/statistics-school-workforce

Education Endowment Foundation (2018), 'Teaching and learning toolkit', https://educationendowmentfoundation.org.uk/evidence-summaries/teaching-learning-toolkit

European Agency for Special Needs and Inclusive Education (2009), 'Multicultural diversity and special needs education'. Odense, Denmark: European Agency for Development in Special Needs Education, www.european-agency.org/resources/publications/multicultural-diversity-and-special-needs-education

Fox, J. D. and Stinnett, T. A. (1996), 'The effects of labeling bias on prognostic outlook for children as a function of diagnostic label and profession', *Psychology in the Schools*, 33, (2), 143–152.

Harari, Y. N. (2015), *Sapiens: A Brief History of Humankind*. London: Vintage.

I CAN help (undated), 'Factsheet: language and mental health', https://ican.org.uk/media/1763/language-and-mental-health.pdf

Iudici, A., Faccio, E., Belloni, E. and Costa, N. (2014), 'The use of the ADHD diagnostic label: what implications exist for children and their families?' *Procedia—Social and Behavioral Sciences*, 122, 506–509.

Kayama, M. and Haight, W. (2018), 'Balancing the stigmatization risks of disability labels against the benefits of special education: Japanese parents' perceptions', *Children and Youth Services Review*, 89, 43–53.

Mahar, A. L., Cobigo, V. and Stuart, H. (2013), 'Conceptualizing belonging', *Disability and Rehabilitation*, 35, (12), 1026–1032.

Maras, K., Marshall, I. and Sands, C. (2019), 'Mock juror perceptions of credibility and culpability in an autistic defendant', *Journal of Autism and Developmental Disorders*, 49, (3), 996–1010.

McMahon, S. E. (2012), 'Doctors diagnose, teachers label: the unexpected in pre-service teachers' talk about labelling children with ADHD', *International Journal of Inclusive Education*, 16, (3), 249–264.

Mehrabian, A. (1972), *Nonverbal Communication*. New Brunswick: Aldine Transaction.

No Isolation (2017), 'How does social isolation affect a child's mental health and development?', www.noisolation.com/global/research/how-does-social-isolation-affect-a-childs-mental-health-and-development

Odell, E. (2019), 'Special or unique: young people's attitudes to disability', www.drilluk.org.uk/wp-content/uploads/2019/08/DR-UK-Special-or-Unique-August-2019.pdf

Ofsted (2019), 'School inspection handbook', www.gov.uk/government/publications/school-inspection-handbook-eif

Ohan, J. L., Visser, T. A. W., Strain, M. C. and Allen, L. (2011), 'Teachers' and education students' perceptions of and reactions to children with and without the diagnostic label "ADHD"', *Journal of School Psychology*, 49, (1), 81–105.

Pesonen, H., Kontu, E., Saarinen, M. and Pirttimaa, R. (2015), 'Conceptions associated with sense of belonging in different school placements for Finnish pupils with special education needs', *European Journal of Special Needs Education*, 31, (1), 59–75.

Rotz, R. and Wright, S. D. (2020), 'The body–brain connection: how fidgeting sharpens focus', *ADDitude*, www.additudemag.com/focus-factors

Royal College of Speech and Language Therapists (2019), 'Improving mental health outcomes for school age children: evidence of links with speech, language and communication', www.rcslt.org/-/media/Project/improving-mental-health-outcomes.pdf

Seidenberg, M. (2017), *Language at the Speed of Sight*. New York, NY: Basic Books.

Shibata, K., Sasaki, Y., Won Bang, J., Walsh, E. G., Machizawa, M. G., Tamaki, M., Chang, L.- H. and Watanabe, T. (2017), 'Overlearning hyperstablizes a skill by rapidly making neurochemical processing inhibitory-dominant', *Nature Neuroscience*, 20, 470–75.

Silberman, S. (2015), *NeuroTribes*. London: Allen & Unwin.

Slee, R. (2019), 'Belonging in an age of exclusion', *International Journal of Inclusive Education*, 23, (9), 909–922.

Standards and Testing Agency (2020), 'Early years foundation stage profile: 2020 handbook', www.gov.uk/government/publications/early-years-foundation-stage-profile-handbook

Staples-Farmer, S. C. (2014), 'Racking up cultural capital and eliminating labels: the culture of teaching and learning in the juvenile justice system', unpublished doctoral dissertation. Lincoln, NE: University of Nebraska.

UK ADHD Partnership (undated), 'ADHD and exclusion in schools', www.ukadhd.com/adhd-and-exclusion-in-schools.htm

Wiliam, D. (2014), 'Dylan Wiliam on feedback', https://blogs.glowscotland.org.uk/wl/deanslearningcommunity/2014/10/31/teaching-and-learning/feedback

Willis, T. (2014), 'The effects of students' gender and EBD labels on teacher acceptability of classroom-based behavioural strategies and teacher self-efficacy', unpublished doctoral dissertation. Commerce, TX: Texas A&M University-Commerce.

Index